40 Days to Awaken Your Sober Mind

LOOK ALIVE, SIS!

JENN KAUTSCH
with Margot Starbuck

Look Alive, Sis: 40 Days to Awaken Your Sober Mind

ISBN: 978-1-95756-604-7

Cover Design by Kelsie Fitzhenry
Interior Design by Niddy Griddy Design, Inc.

LCCN: 2022922180

Printed in the United States of America

1 2 3 4 5 6 7 8 9 10 Printing/Year 27 26 25 24 23

Contents

Acknowledgments

Well, I believe three things in life will last forever, and this book is not one of them. That may be a shocking statement from someone who just poured her heart into something so tangible. However, what *will* last forever is God, His Word, and the hearts of people. I see this work as an investment in people, in *you*. I give God the glory and honor for providing, protecting, and giving me the wisdom and strength to take on this special calling and assignment.

Writing a book is a little like giving birth: pushing, listening to advice, getting support, and leaning on the professionals for delivery.

Every person on the Sober Sis team was a trooper throughout the process. They held space for me when I was overwhelmed and cheered me on the entire time. Kelsie, wow, what a great job you did on the cover! Thank you for all of your patience with me on the back-and-forth until we got it right. Isabel, you are like the rudder to the vessel in turbulent waters. Always calm and pragmatic, seeing the core of the issue at hand, and keeping us all on track and sailing toward the finish line. Stacy, you are such an encouraging comrade, and you always know just what to say to reassure and affirm my efforts. You are my sounding board and a soft place for me to land. Janet, thanks for being there in spirit while you were *actually* giving birth and becoming a new mom throughout this project.

So what about the pros who delivered? Yates and Yates was the engine that connected us to key players. Margot, you are the first editor I've ever worked with, and my experience with you exceeded all of my hopes and expectations. I'm deeply grateful for the countless conversations; your fun-loving input and high energy kept me going. You listened to my heart. This book will bless many, and you arranged and organized my thoughts beautifully. Mike and Karen, your expertise and ability to help us avoid mistakes was so valuable. Together, everyone took the project into overdrive in record time.

Ultimately, this project was years in the making, and my family was there the whole time. Craig, thanks for your vision and for encouraging me to put my experience into words to help others. Katie Jo and Fish, thanks for always believing in me. Mom and Dad, you're the ones who helped launch me from a little girl to the woman I am now. You gave me a steadfast moral compass and an example to follow. Thanks to you, my foundation is rock solid, and thousands of women have borrowed that strength so they could get their own footing.

To all of my fellow sober-minded sisters from around the world, I'm forever grateful to be your humble servant and guide on this journey. Thank you for teaching me along the way. This book is dedicated to you.

Introduction

Hey Sis,

Wherever you find yourself today, this book is for you. Maybe you're at a point where you're considering what sober-minded living could look like in your life. Or maybe you've been on this journey for a while. Wherever you are today, I'm excited to share these forty daily meditations with you.

What I've learned on this journey is that what needs to change, as much as our drinking, is our thinking. A lot of us have been bullied by the old life-draining thoughts in our minds that have been convincing us to drink. And so, part of being renewed, part of living well, is to weed the garden of those old thoughts that haven't served us well. So, we consciously choose to reject those old thoughts and replace them with new ones that are life giving. And that's why, as I wrote, I imagined each of these meditations as a seed that you can plant in your garden. Each day I'll share one of these seeds, a key idea, and I'll also unpack that idea by reflecting on it a bit. My hope is that these seeds will take root in the garden of your mind and nourish your heart on this journey. And, on every page, I'm hoping you'll know that I am with you. Our community is with you. As you commit to a life of flourishing, you are not alone.

Keep going and growing,
Jenn

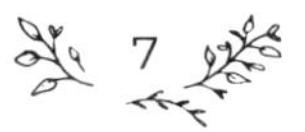

We don't have to live at the
whim of our desires.
We can change them.

What Do You *Really* Want?

It had been a very stressful morning. Very. Stressful. *You feel me?* Entering the grocery store, I opened up my shopping list on my phone and grabbed my cart, and the first thing I saw when I stopped inside was an attractive wine display. Thinking how nice it would be to have a glass while I'm cooking that evening, I decided to pick up a bottle for later. Then my hubs and I would share the rest over dinner.

It's all good. It's all above board. It all makes sense.

Well, when I read the promotion, I discovered that there's a "special": two bottles for the price of one. (I mean, you can't decline the *special*. It would basically be throwing money down the toilet.) So, I grabbed the white I'd had my eye on and a red to share with company the following evening. Smart girl!

When I got home, I popped open the white and poured a glass before putting it into the fridge. I mean, it's 5-*ish*, and I'll be standing in the kitchen for the next hour. It will

sustain me. One glass, before my husband came home, turned into two. (He was running late. So me drinking that second glass was on him.) After he came home, we all had dinner, and then he and I cuddled up on the couch to watch a movie. By the end of the movie, we'd opened the second bottle. You know how it goes.

Rather than being mindful, I was being driven by my *desires*. I never would have admitted that at the moment, but I was.

The reality was that I had competing desires: I wanted to drink. I didn't want to drink. If you picture a little white cartoon angel over one shoulder and a little red cartoon devil over the other, those two were in constant conflict. And when you're caught between those competing desires, you are more than likely going to choose the drink! It's just the way our brains are designed, the pathways we've built over time (plus savvy marketing), and the nature of alcohol. It's not that you and I are "broken" or extremely flawed or weak, but when we're conflicted like that, our brains are doing what they've been trained to do. It's a pattern that needs rewiring.

When I came to this insight, it felt so liberating. If the rare topic of drinking was ever brought up in religious culture, I'd been taught that it was solely an issue of the heart. But what I learned was that it's actually a brain-wiring issue. As a neuroscientist, Dr. Caroline Leaf has given me a holistic perspective. Dr. Leaf says, "Thoughts are located in three different places: in your brain, in your mind, and in the cells of your body." (Caroline Leaf, *Cleaning Up Your Mental Mess. Grand Rapids, MI:* Baker Books, 2021, 140.)

We don't have to live at the whim of our desires. We can change them. In the Christian faith, we'd say that you're changed "by the renewing of your mind" (Romans 12:2). And when our *minds* change, our *desires* change. I've experienced it firsthand, and you can too. So, you may just decide you want to cut back on your drinking and have less of it. Or you may decide you don't feel like you need it or even want it anymore. Either way, lasting change happens from the inside out—starting with your mind.

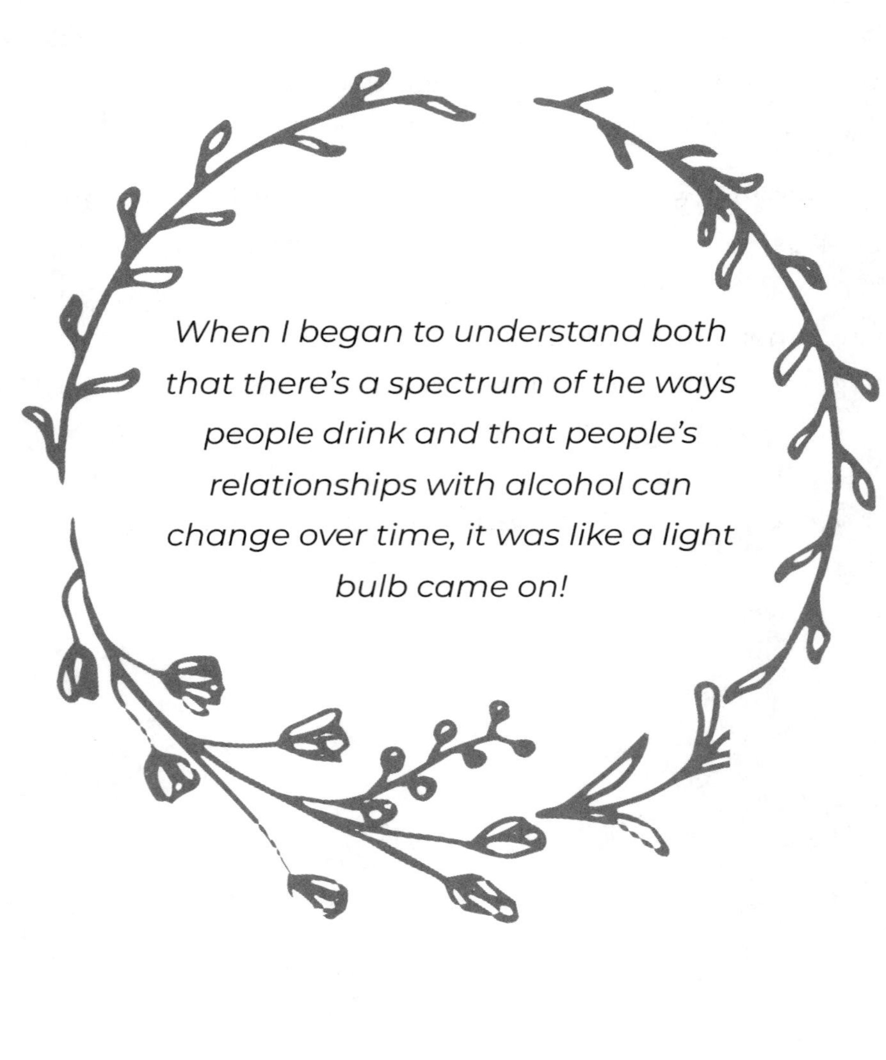

When I began to understand both that there's a spectrum of the ways people drink and that people's relationships with alcohol can change over time, it was like a light bulb came on!

The Gray Area

You know how there's that moment in *The Wizard of Oz* when Dorothy lands in Oz and her world changes from black-and-white to full Technicolor? That was awesome, right? And it's a little bit like how I felt when my life shifted from black-and-white to gray.

Let me explain.

The way I was showing up in my own life was less than what I was made for. I was pretending that I was "lighthearted" when at times I was actually "heavyhearted." When sipping on my vino during wine o'clock, I was pretending I had it all together when really, I felt a disconnect—within myself and with the people around me. I was internally suffering from a divided mind: one that was mindful by day only to become "mindless" after five o'clock.

My life had become something I wouldn't have recognized years earlier. And that was due, in part, to the black-and-white thinking I'd fallen into—specifically, around alcohol.

At the time I understood that some people were *not* alcoholics; other people were.

The label "alcoholic" can set up this dichotomy that says either you're a "normal" drinker or you're an "alcoholic." Short of being a teetotaler, those were the two options. This kind of black-and-white thinking says that either you have a problem or you don't. And if you haven't lost your job, home, spouse, and kids because of your drinking, you don't need to change.

Sis, that thinking is pretty problematic! And it's kept a lot of us stuck.

The truth is that there's a pretty wide spectrum when it comes to the ways people drink. So, to insist that someone either wears the "alcoholic" label or doesn't neglects the reality that people's relationship with alcohol typically changes over time and across contexts. People tend to drink more, not less, over time. That's because alcohol is an addictive substance and actually creates a thirst for itself! Our tolerance rises and so does our craving for more in order to get the same effect. This is actually our brains and bodies performing on a normal psychological level. Now let's add in the social and emotional layers. So many people have remarked to me, "You know, alcohol was never really an issue for me, and then this thing happened." Or they'll notice, "My drinking changed when my kids left for college." Or they might observe, "When I lost someone really close, I started drinking more."

When I began to understand both that there's a spectrum of the ways people drink and that people's relationships with alcohol can change over time, it was like a light bulb came on! I was finally able to recognize that black-and-white thinking—insisting either you're a skid row alcoholic or you've got zero problems with drinking—wasn't helping me. Or anyone.

Dorothy's reality shifted from black-and-white to Technicolor. But my reality began to change when I shifted from black-and-white thinking to discovering that my drinking was somewhere between black and white—it was in the *gray* zone.

Discovering this "gray zone"—where I could finally admit that alcohol was interfering with my life—was a game changer for me. It might be for you too.

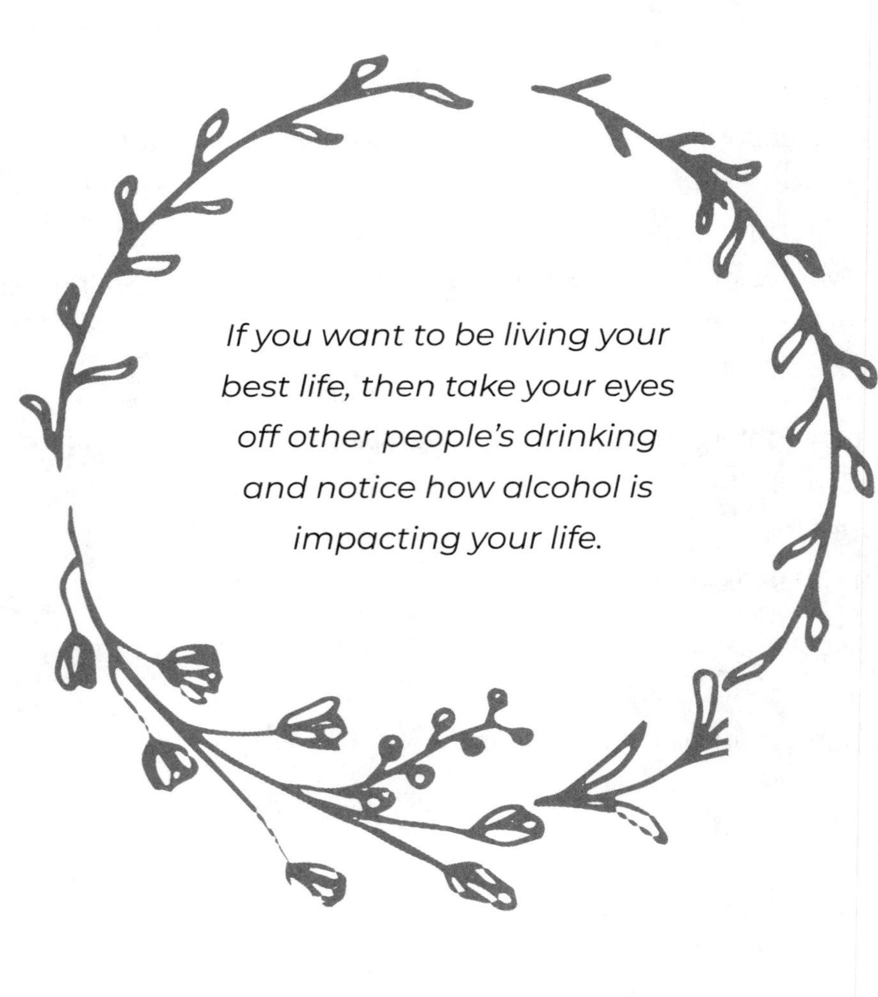

If you want to be living your best life, then take your eyes off other people's drinking and notice how alcohol is impacting your life.

The Comparison Trap

Monday evenings meant one thing to my friend Jackie: *Bring Your Own Bottle* book club. That's when the women in her neighborhood were gathering to discuss *The Glass Castle* or whatever Brené Brown's most recent wonder might be. But the vino did sweeten the deal! It was the one evening each week when Jackie got to leave the kids at home with their dad and enjoy her girls.

As she slowly sipped her first glass, Jackie would feel herself relax into playfulness and fun. Her gaze would wander around the circle, noticing how many glasses the other women were drinking. Inevitably she'd pause on Candice, who'd been sampling from OWB (Other Women's Bottles). One. Two. Three. Four. Yeah, Jackie was counting.

Jackie did the same thing on family vacations with her husband's side of the family. Because if her sister-in-law had more to drink than Jackie did, then *she* obviously didn't have a problem. Her sister-in-law? Now *she* might

have a problem. And Candice from the book club? It seemed like she really might be a problem drinker.

You see what's up, right? We comfort ourselves, we justify our drinking choices, when we can find *one person in the room* who's drinking more than we are. If we can find that one person, then we can convince ourselves that it's not that bad. That we don't have a problem.

Comparison is a trap. And being a little "better" than the worst person is going to keep us stuck.

Here's the deal. Think about it, do you drink more or less than you did when you first started drinking? I'm talking about the amount and how often. I remember, at the beginning, when one glass of pink Zinfandel would make me feel like a noodle. But over time, I built up a tolerance. And I thought that was a *good* thing!

If you want to get free, you need to keep your eyes on *you*. The amount that someone else is or isn't drinking really has nothing to do with you. Rather than convincing yourself that you're "not as bad" as *she* is, there are better questions you can be asking.

- Are my relationships at home affected by my drinking?
- Are my drinking habits keeping me stuck emotionally?

- Is my alcohol consumption interfering with my sleep or my health?
- Has drinking become a coping mechanism for my anxiety?

If you want to be living your best life, then take your eyes off other people's drinking and notice how alcohol is impacting *your life*. Because there are always going to be people who drink less than you. And if you really try, you'll always find people who drink more than you. Any way you slice it, comparison keeps you stuck.

Alcohol will never deliver what it is that we most want and need.

Alcohol's Insufficiency

Carrie Bradshaw, from *Sex and the City*, made drinking look *fantastic*. Am I right? The stylish writer sipping a cosmo at a crowded bar was the essence of glamour and sophistication. And whether we've been changing diapers, hustling at work, or hassling teens to unload the dishwasher, Carrie Bradshaw was living the life anyone would want. She was young. She was attractive. She was successful. She was surrounded by her girls. Who wouldn't want that life?!

Now, I'm not going to say that we *consciously* believe a mix of vodka, liqueur, and a few fruity juices is going to secure all that Carrie had, but . . . who could fault us if we hoped a little bit? Alcohol manufacturers have poured millions of dollars into convincing us that alcohol is going to make our lives better. Their ads feature happy, fit, sexy, attractive people having fun and relaxing with their friends. There's even the suggestion that this is where we'll be known and accepted for who we are. And who wouldn't want that?

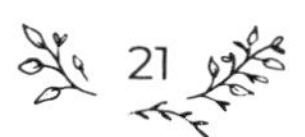

The problem is that these advertisers are making a promise on which alcohol can never deliver. The reality isn't nearly as pretty as Carrie and the girls made it seem.

> Alcohol is addictive.
> Alcohol makes us feel awful the next day.
> Alcohol robs us of energy.
> Alcohol disrupts our sleep.
> Alcohol causes weight gain.
> Alcohol costs money we may or may not have to waste.
> Alcohol steals our time.
> Alcohol sabotages our goals.
> Alcohol fuels cancer cells.
> Alcohol dehydrates.
> Alcohol adds to our stress levels.

For decades, alcohol advertising targeted men. And to do that, their no-brainer ads used women. They'd sprinkle some beautiful women among the guys drinking at a bar or a Super Bowl party, and the product would fly off the shelves. That works for men. Now, women are a little more complex than men, and sexy cabana boys delivering martinis only works for a small sliver of the market.

But these savvy marketers figured out that women also had dollars to spend on alcohol. And they do know how to reach us. So they show us beautiful women connecting socially with one another. (I want that, don't you?) And they put these enticing displays as close to the checkout lane in the grocery store as they can get 'em. They catch us with our guard down, with a fun-labeled bottle of Pinot Grigio that's as easy to grab as the Reese's Peanut Butter Cups!

They're marketing geniuses.

But why don't you and I agree on one thing right now: alcohol can't deliver on the promises that advertisers make to convince us to turn over our dollars to them.

It doesn't make us more attractive; it makes us gain weight.

It doesn't make us "feel better"; okay . . . for an hour or two it does, but ultimately it makes us feel worse.

It doesn't enhance our relationships; it complicates our relationships.

When we're sober-minded, we know all these things. So let's keep telling each other the truth, Sis.

Alcohol will never deliver what it is that we most want and need.

God always works with what is real.

You're Not Alone

"It's good to be reminded that you were all once just like me," I read on one post in our private Sober Sis community. The newcomer continued, "I'm not alone."

This, I thought to myself, *is exactly why we exist.*

"God is always here," she admitted, "but tangible sisters are making a huge difference for me."

At Sober Sis, we're convinced that to make and sustain any positive change in your life, it really does take a village. And what makes this group a little different than a lot of the communities we might already be a part of—our families, our churches, our friend groups—is that we've cultivated an environment where it's safe to reveal yourself. It's a place where you can experience being both known and loved.

Did you catch the last part in that sister's testimony? That even though God is here, we still need others? I believe that God *is* here for us—for me, for you—but there's also something about the tangible experience of journeying with other women that anchors us and helps us along the way. And I believe that it's by God's good design! I think it's what the church is supposed to be like: a community void of judgment where we can be honest about who we really are. But too often we've failed.

Some churches have become places where we're only willing to show our best selves. Whether we show up in a new dress or our favorite jeans, stepping through the doors of a church can make some of us feel like we've got to "look good." And so, we smile. We chitchat. When someone asks us how we are, we don't even consider telling them the truth. Instead, we assure others that we're *good*. That it's all *good*.

We might feel this way in other social groups too—with fellow baseball moms or at corporate parties. We are "in the club" as long as we act and fit the part. But a community with conditions is not an authentic community. We do it on social media too, showing others the "filtered" pictures of our lives—cropping out the empty wine bottles, concealing our thought-consuming obsession with drinking, and hiding the wasted time and the heartache. Our inauthenticity doesn't give God anything to work with. God always works with what is *real.*

What's real is being honest about the highs and lows of our journeys.

What's real is showing others who we are, *as we are*, without posturing.

What's real is *sharing* our journeys without *comparing* our journeys.

What's real is receiving another's story without any judgment.

What's real is coming alongside another sister to encourage her, right where she is, rather than trying to "fix" her.

And that's why it's been so exciting to see God build this vibrant, empowered sisterhood where we're learning how to show up for one another. How to be present with one another. When one of us falls, we pick her up, dust her off, and set her back on the path. And every single day I see evidence that we are stronger together.

Beloved Sister, *you are not alone*. The community is here for you.

All of our relationships are better when we're sober-minded.

Deeper Connection

When I heard the front door open and shut, I peeked at my phone to check the time. Yeah, I'm that mom who's waiting to know that my kids have made it home from a Friday night football game or a date. And he made it in before curfew.

"Hey, dude," I said. "How'd it go?"

Plopping down on the couch beside me, he gave me the scoop on his date. I tried to act pretty cool, but inside I was pumped to be hearing about it.

I wish it wasn't the case, but there were those weekend nights—late at night, after a few glasses of wine—when I just wasn't *fully* present for my kids. Groggy, I was still able to check the time as I heard them walk in for curfew, but I wasn't able to be as available to them as I would have liked after a certain hour.

So there's the *regular* "mom" part of me who's delighted that my son is willing to share with me. And today there's also the *sober-minded* "mom" part of me who is grateful

not to be missing those tiny moments with my kids because I've been drinking.

The same is true in my marriage. Every marriage is going to have those issues which come up throughout the day that need to be resolved. But when our brains are hijacked by any substance, it's hard to resolve those pent-up frustrations and disagreements. When we're half out of it, we lose the *healthy* filter that helps us choose to use our words well.

All of our relationships are better when we're sober-minded.

Even your relationship with yourself improves. Before I was living truly sober-minded, as someone totally present in my own life, I was buzzing through life divided. Even when I wasn't conscious of it, there was an internal conflict within myself. And the same skills that were needed to connect with my kids and my husband—the ability to be fully present, to manage big feelings, to use my best words—are the same sober-minded skills I needed to have a healthy relationship *with myself*.

In the Bible, in a letter that a guy named Paul wrote to a group of people who were a lot like us, he explained, "For God has not given us a spirit of fear, but of power and of love and of a sound mind" (2 Timothy 1:7). And in language that we'd use today, I'd say that what he's describing is a *sober* mind.

When we encounter chaos during a pandemic, when we face tricky situations in our homes, and when we're stressed about work, what we most need is that sound and sober mind. And when we cultivate that sober mind, when we choose not to let alcohol disrupt our peace, our relationships benefit because we're fully present to our people, better able to connect with others and ourselves.

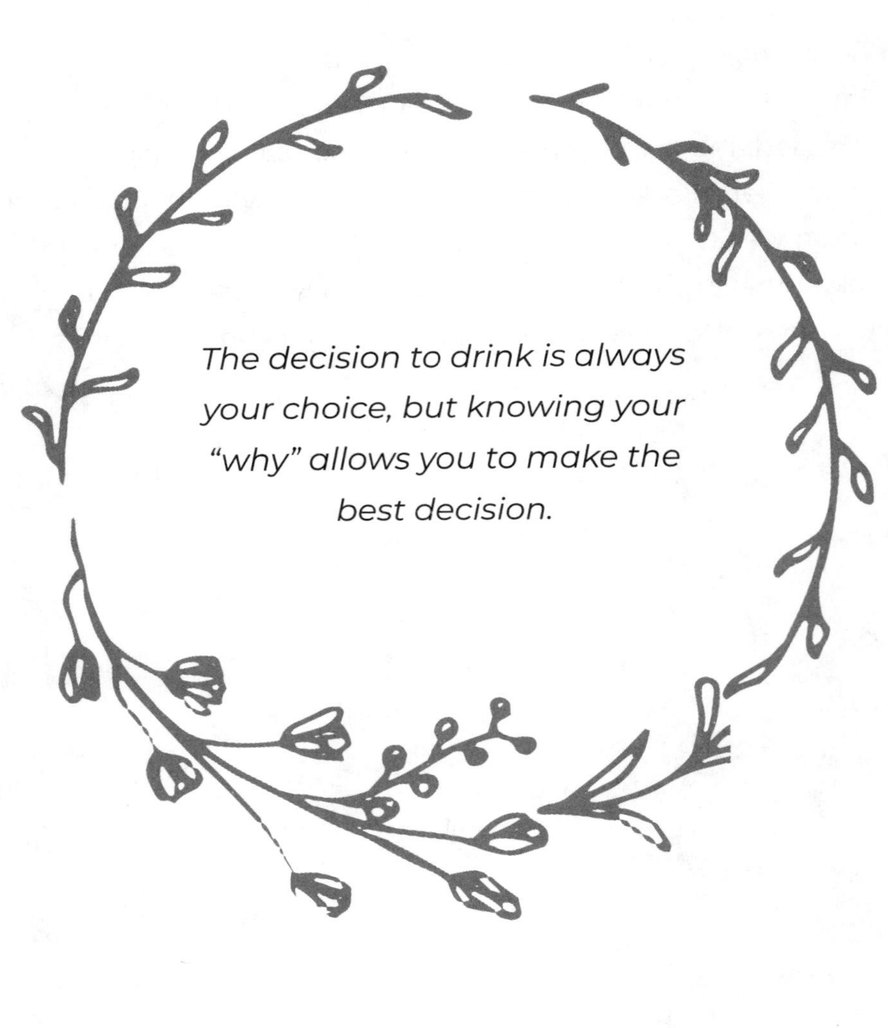
The decision to drink is always your choice, but knowing your "why" allows you to make the best decision.

Knowing Your "Why"

When a woman chooses to engage in Sober Sis's 21 Day Reset Challenge, she might feel a little nervous about it. It's the beginning of a hike into the unknown, and even though she's got her gear and her girls, there's a part of her that's not sure she's got the stamina to complete it.

And that's why the very first thing I ask of this brave adventurer is to do this one simple thing:

Make a list of every reason you drink.

I ask her to dig deep to discover the compelling "why" that causes her to drink. And that's because discovering this "why"—and eventually answering the "why" of *why* she does *not* want to drink—is what's going to propel her on this journey. In the hard moments she's going to remember both the reasons why she drinks and also the reasons why she may choose not to drink.

Sister, I want you to pause now to consider your *why*.

To grease the wheels, I'll share what some women have named as the reasons they drink:

- It helps me relax.
- It feels social and festive.
- I feel I deserve it. I've *earned* it.
- It helps me fit in.

How about you? What's on your list? You may have three or four reasons, or there may be dozens on your list! That's fine. The conscious beliefs, like the ones I mentioned, will likely bubble up to the surface first. But I encourage you to dig deeper. Look for the reasons that might be hiding under the surface.

- It numbs old pain.
- It distracts me from what's happening in my family in this season.
- It soothes the cutting comment he tossed out this morning.

The reason this part of the journey is so critical is because even when your conscious mind wants to drink less, or even quit altogether, your unconscious mind believes that you need to keep drinking for some very good reasons. These reasons need to be brought into the light, evaluated, and maybe even challenged. Ask yourself, are they even true?

So now that you've brought your conscious and unconscious beliefs to the surface, we can shine a light on them and examine them, and you can decide for yourself whether the reasons you drink are valid enough for you to keep drinking.

The decision to drink is always your choice, but knowing your "why" allows you to make the best decision.

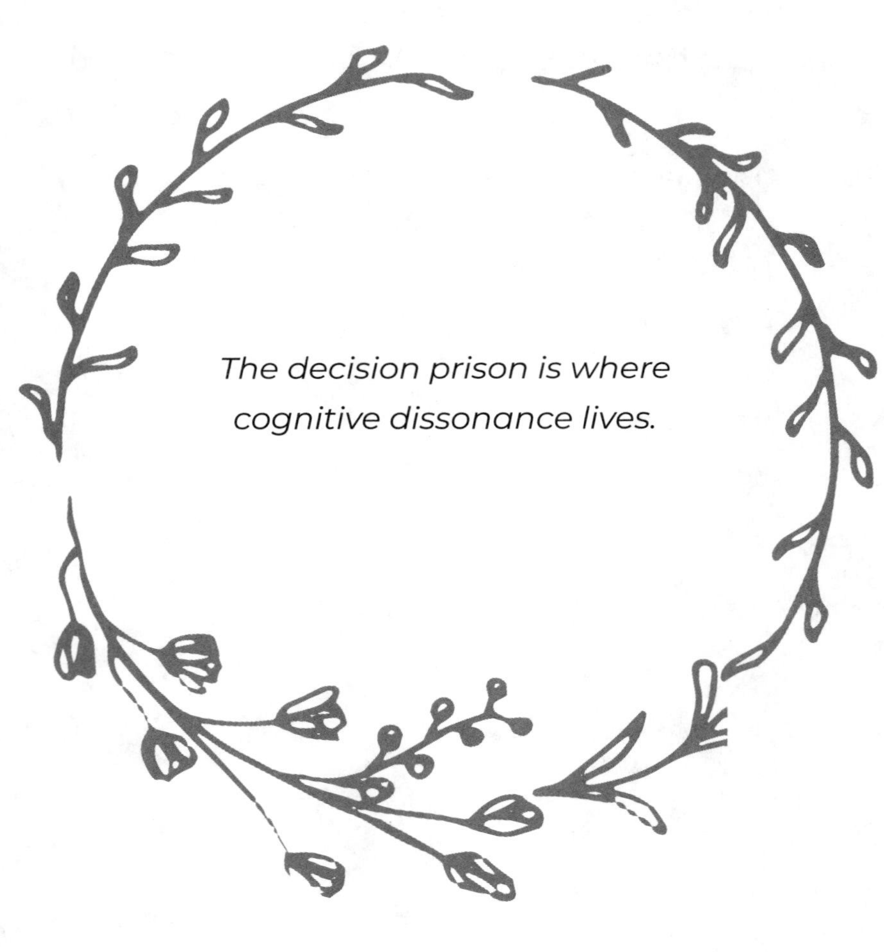

The decision prison is where cognitive dissonance lives.

Moderation

"Why not just practice moderation?"

This is what I hear from people who are curious why I choose not to drink alcohol.

So I give them a peek into my story and tell them, "I could moderate."

I notice the person for whom this question was so important breathes a sigh of relief.

And then I add, *"Until I couldn't."*

That's my story.

I believe some people find that moderation works for them: either alcohol has not become that important to them, so drinking less is easy, *or* they are willing to take the time and effort to make it work.

I've been living the alcohol-free lifestyle since April 2017, and it has been what's worked best for me. The problem is that moderation requires *management*. What that means is it requires attention, vigilance, and multiple decision filters. It takes bandwidth in my mind. When I was making those little decisions all day long—to be clear: pretty good decisions in the mornings, but harder to follow through as the day would turn into evening—it didn't feel like freedom. It felt like a decision prison.

The decision prison is where cognitive dissonance lives. Cognitive dissonance requires a ton of mental calories that I could use in more productive ways. During my moderation days, I could never stop the back-and-forth ping-pong game in my head that was consuming my mind. Thinking about drinking or not drinking, all day long, requires a lot of mental gymnastics. This is why the alcohol-free lifestyle is my path of choice. This one single decision I've made helps me to avoid the decision prison.

I want you to make the best choice for you, without judgment from me, but I also want you to be aware of the risks and realities you have to consider with the moderation monster. What's tricky about moderation is that it's *conditional*. It depends on the "conditions" of my, and your, emotional state and sometimes our physical environment.

Am I sad?

Am I overwhelmed?

Am I getting along with those around me?

Do I want to be at this event?

Do I feel alone?

For me, while I was in the moderation world, the "eject button" was too handy. Reaching for a drink was just too easy. You might feel similarly. You might sense that moderation is simply a justification for keeping the door open for those hard and heavy nights when you want to run back to alcohol for rescue.

This past summer my family lost our sweet dog Franklin. It was painful, but because I was alcohol-free, I was able to show up with resilience. But the first time our family lost a dog, over a decade ago, I was a real train wreck. I'd never been through a grief like that, and so I suppressed the sadness, which kept me stuck in it so much longer! Although it's a little counterintuitive, we're able to feel our grief and move on when we are free to feel the feels. When we encounter bumps in the road—the diagnosis, the bad news, the natural disaster—moderation may fail us.

Living alcohol-free feels better because I can be available to the people I love 24-7.

Feeling Your Best

Here's something men never have to consider: when you're feeling tipsy or even three sheets to the wind, no one's thinking about taking off her makeup. (Sisters, I know you feel me on this one.)

In a long list of reasons why living alcohol-free just *feels* better, this one definitely makes my top ten list. I know, I know, there are more *noble* reasons, but every day I wake up and see a pillowcase that's not smeared with mascara and lipstick, I'm reminded that today I'm so much healthier than I was six years ago. Being alert enough to embrace my evening routine of taking off my makeup and brushing my teeth before bedtime is just a little signpost reminding me that living alcohol-free feels better.

Living alcohol-free feels better because I can be available to the people I love 24-7. The choice to be alcohol-free is often a unique and complicated recipe for each woman, but part of the catalyst that motivated me to stop drinking was that my daughter, at nineteen, moved from our home in Texas to San Francisco. Her move was a big deal for

of us! With California in a different time zone, it was hours earlier than the time in Texas, and I wanted to be available to her if she called during her early- and late-evening hours.

A couple of years into my alcohol-free lifestyle, I got a phone call that my son had broken his arm skateboarding at 10 p.m. And it didn't escape me that if I'd gotten that call a number of years back, I would have struggled to stay calm and articulate at the ER, let alone be present and useful there until 3 a.m. Living alcohol-free feels better.

Beyond the clean pillowcases and showing up fully present, living alcohol-free has had countless wins for me:

- ✓ I sleep better.
- ✓ I have more energy.
- ✓ I eat healthier.
- ✓ My workouts are better.
- ✓ I wake up clearheaded.
- ✓ I have more dollars in my pocket.

Some of us haven't even paused to consider whether our "normal"—the slight headache, the dull fog, the sapped energy—is what "normal" should or could be! Often when we pause to consider our drinking, we ask, "Is it bad enough?" *Has it gotten bad enough for me to stop*? But I want to encourage you to flip the question. Ask yourself, "Is it *good* enough?" If you haven't paused to imagine how your life might be better without alcohol, it's worth stopping—right now—and *really* asking yourself this question.

The first half of my forties were the toughest years of my life, both as a mom and as a person. I was surviving, but I wasn't *thriving*. Today, though? Living alcohol-free? I feel better from the moment I wake up with that clean pillowcase to the moment I drop off to a (mostly) sound sleep, knowing that I've been able to be present to my people. Every single day, living alcohol-free feels better.

You were made
for freedom, too.

Made for Freedom

I fall onto the sofa after a full day of lunch making, volunteering, grocery shopping, carpool driving, soccer shuttling, and dinner prep. Hubby is out at a meeting, and I'm ready to chill. After all, I've *earned* it. I've set a glass of wine on the end table—as if I'll stop at one glass. But I have the quiet comfort of knowing that the fresh bottle is available on the kitchen counter. Grabbing the remote, I click on my favorite show and settle in for "me time." (Because it's my "reward," remember?) I tell myself I'm living in freedom, but there's a part of me that knows I'm not.

Because I'm functioning on autopilot, I'm not being intentional about the difference I want to make in the world. Honestly, I'm having a hard time seeing past what's right in front of me. Throughout the day, as the clock ticked toward wine o'clock, the good intentions I'd had midmorning seemed to evaporate.

After a day of eating kale and sweating through a ninety-minute hot yoga class, I am pouring every saved or burned calorie, and more, straight down my throat.

Night after night, I've been chasing a fleeting feeling, trying to satisfy my desires.

I miss the last twenty minutes of the show because, well . . . you know, I'll just say I wasn't entirely alert.

And, frankly, I'm weary of repeating this cycle that feels more like bondage than freedom.

Now fast-forward. It's been another full day, but now I am five years into alcohol-free living, a personal choice I decided to make for countless reasons.

For starters, I woke up from a full night's sleep feeling well rested. (Wait, what?!) Yup, it's true.

I was clear-minded enough to want to use what I've been given to impact the world for good—and I actually seized an opportunity to do it.

I saved 500 wasted calories my body didn't need. (Did I still stop for a Dairy Queen mini-Blizzard? Yeah, I did. #winning)

Did I have extra money after not buying wine and wholeheartedly buying my ice cream? I did. I really did.

And I caught the *entire* episode of *This Is Us*. Not to be a show-off, but I can tell you everything that happened. Not just the stuff before glass-o-vino #2.

So let's break it down. For years I'd convinced myself that I was in control. That everyone was drinking like I was. That I deserved it. That I was free. But the part of me that so desperately wanted to believe that wasn't the clear-minded part. It was the cloudy part that was being bullied by my desires. And when I was finally able to see clearly, because I was alcohol-free, I was able to recognize what bondage was and what freedom was.

I'm not gonna lie: it's fantastic. Today I'm clear-minded not just for the first dozen or so hours of my day. I'm in my right mind for *all of them*. I'm able to be present for myself and others. I feel good. I make choices from a place of freedom and not bondage.

You were made for freedom, too.

You have everything it takes to make a mindful choice.

Playing It Forward

Let me give you a peek at the opening scene of two different short films.

In the first film, Maria races from work, to the grocery store, to day care. When they get home, the kids play in the yard while Maria sets the table for dinner. As she does, she sees the bottle of wine her in-laws brought by the night before.

In the second film, Maria races from work, to the grocery store, to day care. When they get home, the kids play in the yard while Maria sets the table for dinner. As she does, she sees the bottle of wine her in-laws brought by the night before.

In the first film, Maria hasn't really made a plan about whether or not she'll drink. So before throwing ingredients for her famous veggie chili into a pot on the stove, she opens a bottle of wine she swiped near the checkout lane at the grocery store. Though she *sees* the bottle of wine her in-laws brought by the night before, she knows

that it's "accounted for." Someone may ask about it. The impulse purchase, though? It can be her little secret. (Especially if she wraps it in a paper bag and disposes of it in the *garbage*, instead of in the recycling bin, exposed for any person to stumble across.)

In the second film, Maria has made a mindful choice not to drink. In the morning, she stocked the crockpot with the ingredients for her famous veggie chili. She pre-decided and she had a plan. At the grocery store, Maria grabbed her favorite kombucha, and she popped it in the fridge to stay chilled. So while the kids play in the yard, Maria stretches her legs and clears her head by walking around the block a couple of times. She pre-decided. She had a plan that didn't involve lingering alone in the kitchen. She'd set up the evening for success.

Now I want you to do something called "playing the movie forward." When you play the movie forward, you anticipate what will likely happen in the movie. It's not that you're a wizard; it's that you know what usually happens in this movie. And so you can predict with a very high degree of accuracy how it will end.

For example, in the first movie Maria knows that once she opens that bottle, she will *finish* that bottle—either publicly or privately. In this movie she lies wide awake in bed at 3 a.m. with dread, anxiety, and a racing heartbeat.

The next day she wakes up with a dull headache and a foggy brain.

In the second movie—the one where Maria would have enjoyed some wine, except she made a mindful choice to stay sober-minded—the plan she put into action meant that she reduced the temptation of lingering alone in the kitchen; she got some exercise; she enjoyed her family at dinner; she slept soundly; and she awoke the next morning refreshed.

You have everything it takes to make a mindful choice. You can choose, ahead of time, not to drink alcohol. You already know what happens in the movie where you come home from the store with a bottle of Chardonnay and spend an hour alone in the kitchen. You know how it ends! So instead of playing that old show on repeat, set yourself up for success by pre-planning.

You'll love how that movie ends.

I haven't found alcohol to have enough value to cause me to bring it back into my life again.

Choosing Change

"Today I drink as much as I want, when I want," I announce.

"Wait, wait," says the Sober Sis newcomer, with more than a little distress in her voice. "I thought you were alcohol-free. I thought that you do *not* drink alcohol. Was I misled? Have I come to the wrong place? Is this not where I can find help?"

I understand her distress. And that's why I want to talk about *wanting*. I want to talk about *desire*. Because I hear how, at first blush, it's a bit counterintuitive.

If you'd told me a decade ago that I didn't have to live with the desire to drink, that I wouldn't *want* to drink, I would not have believed you. (Logically, I *should* have believed you, since I lived for years, prior to drinking, without a desire to drink. I didn't even start drinking socially on a regular basis until my young thirties.)

At the beginning of my alcohol-free journey—which is different from the times I'd "white-knuckled it," using all the willpower I had while taking long and short breaks from drinking alcohol—I very much wanted alcohol. I desired it. And that *desire* had been cultivated by a number of factors.

The alcohol-friendly culture around me had, in part, encouraged me to desire alcohol.

The multibillion-dollar alcohol industry had, in part, persuaded me to want alcohol.

The way alcohol took the edge off, and made me feel—for a moment—not so bad, also encouraged me to crave alcohol.

But on this journey, I've done a lot of inner work. I've committed myself to staying present with my feelings and learning from them. I've done a lot of research to learn how brains and bodies are impacted by alcohol. I've heard from some great teachers. But my decision to remain alcohol-free largely boils down to one thing: *I haven't found alcohol to have enough value to cause me to bring it back into my life again.*

Do you hear what I'm saying? Today, I could make the decision to have a drink. But the reason I don't is because—with a sober mind—I've weighed the pros and cons, the benefits and deficits. And the joy of this journey

has been discovering that life is better, for me, without alcohol. It's why I don't feel deprived every day!

I have lost my desire to drink. My cravings are gone. Yes, it took a while for that to happen, but over time my *mind* began to change. My brain literally changed. And when my mind changed, my *desires* changed. Yours can too.

So today, if you are triggered by emotions, what can you move to the top of your go-to list for relief? Is it taking a hot bath, journaling, enjoying some chocolate, or calling a friend? Over time, I promise you will no longer be bullied by your desires. You'll experience this freedom as a miracle.

You don't have to do all the things all at once.

The Next Step

Alcohol is subtly keeping Sarah from her best life.

Although she hasn't admitted it to anyone, Sarah has begun to notice that her drinking is beginning to disrupt her relationships, her physical health, and even her work-from-home career as a freelance artist. She's got an inner knowing that something needs to change but is not exactly sure what that looks like. Sarah isn't feeling that a twelve-step program is the solution for her. The approach doesn't really resonate with her, and it seems like it's a better fit for further down the drinking spectrum anyway. A friend told her about Sober Sis, but Sarah isn't sure that alcohol-free living is for her. She's pretty sure that never drinking again might be a bit extreme. So Sarah stays stuck.

I would love to sit at a table across from Sarah, sipping a warm vanilla latte, look her in the eye, and assure her, "Girlfriend, take a deep breath. You have a lot of options. And the good news is *that you do not have to do all the things*. Maybe you check out a Celebrate Recovery meeting. Maybe you join us at Sober Sis and check it out.

Heck, maybe you go to therapy! But here's what we know for sure: you don't have to do all the things; you only have to do the *next* thing."

And suddenly Sarah can *breathe* again.

It can feel daunting for any of us to consider a future that interferes with us drinking what we want whenever we want. (Can I get an *amen*?) Of course, that feels scary. And at Sober Sis, we encourage every woman to find what works best for her. And the way to do that is to take the next step.

For one woman, her first brave step is to invite a friend over to eat carrot cake and tell the truth about her drinking. The antidote to addiction is connection, and when she connects with this friend, she exposes what she's experiencing in the dark to the light of day.

For one woman, her next step is to read the copy of this book that her sister "accidentally" left on her coffee table. (Maybe that's you. Right now.)

For one woman, her next step is to join in the next 21 Day Reset Challenge—where she abstains from alcohol for three weeks. It's not going to solve everything by any means, but it's a great start. On this adventure she might have a few slips, but she experiences growth simply by embracing the challenge. It begins to even change the way she looks at alcohol, and that's a win!

Another woman, who's in the Sober Sis community, goes to a family wedding and gets caught up in the moment and drinks after almost seven months of alcohol-free living. The next morning, she connects online with her Sisters, where she finds compassion and support to return to alcohol-free living.

Beloved, the journey to live a sober-minded and authentic life is going to be unique to every woman. You don't have to do all the things all at once. Today, you only need to take your next step.

You've got this, Sis.

She could exercise healthy boundaries and stay true to the person she'd made a decision to be: someone who was sober-minded 24-7.

Healthy Boundaries

At her twentieth college reunion, Keisha met up with her sorority sisters at a local bar and restaurant near campus. After parking her car, she walked across the parking lot toward the terrace where the music was thumping and the girls were already on their first round!

Approaching the bar, Keisha noticed a familiar chatter in her head that she hadn't heard in a while. In the past six months, the voices in her head had become quieter. But she remembered the voices:

"Don't be a buzzkill. We're here to have fun!"

"Just have one. One won't hurt."

"Don't let them down by not drinking. You *owe* them. They're your girls!"

"My friend Donna didn't drink in college, and her social life suffered."

"This is a special occasion! You haven't seen some of these gals for two decades!"

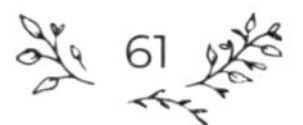

"Just do it. Just drink."

The force and volume of the voices surprised Keisha.

When her bestie, Chantelle, caught sight of Keisha, she hollered, "Keisha's here! Now the party can get started!"

Her reputation lived on.

Keisha made the rounds, hugging and greeting her friends. As she sat down at the bar, she asked the bartender for a glass of water and a virgin frozen daiquiri. Settling in, she listened to snippets of conversations buzzing around her.

One woman protested, "I really shouldn't drink since I have to drive, but one won't hurt."

Another moaned, "I promised my husband I wouldn't drink; we're way over budget every month and trying to tighten our extra spending. But it's not like I'm *not* going to drink with y'all!"

And one woman explained, "When I left home tonight, I'd planned not to drink since I'm nursing. But I'll text my husband. There's breast milk in the freezer."

Another woman chided her friend, "Girl! You're *not* drinking a Diet Coke tonight. I did not fly across the country for that. It's a reunion like old times!"

As she listened to her friends navigating and narrating their own choices about drinking alcohol, Keisha realized that she wasn't alone in having a complicated relationship with alcohol. Slipping into the bathroom, she texted a Sober Sis friend just to share that she was in a tricky situation and confessed that she felt like she "owed" it to her friends.

When the chat bubbles of her friend's reply turned to text, Keisha read, "Don't make a decision for anyone else but you. They won't be in your hotel room bathroom tonight with your head spinning! Make the choice that's right for you. You got this, Sis."

The reply made Keisha smile. And it reminded her of what's most real. She *could* exercise healthy boundaries and stay true to the person she'd made a decision to be: someone who was sober-minded 24-7. And that night her choice to remain alcohol-free exposed the lie that she was somehow disappointing or abandoning her girls by not partaking in that aspect of the party. Instead, because she made the choice that was right for her—to remain alcohol-free—she was actually able to be a friend who could listen better, remember details of the whole night, and *still* have fun dancing.

When you remove alcohol from your life, replace it with something better.

Filling the Void

Researchers from New York University discovered that a craving for alcohol can be tempered by the power of prayer. I love a holistic approach and get excited when the mind/body/spirit connection intersects with science! Their research showed that prayer and meditation can minimize alcohol cravings by stimulating parts of the brain that are responsible for attention and emotion.

When you make the decision to eliminate alcohol from your life—whether for a brief experiment, for a season, or for longer—there's a void where alcohol used to live. But you don't have to walk around on *empty*! Instead, the big win is on filling the space with better, healthier alternatives.

Now, I'm going to share some of these with you, but I need you to agree with me about something first: this is not a to-do list. This isn't putting more on your plate. These options are opportunities for you to replace alcohol with healthy alternatives. You have to find what works for you!

- Walk outside. I'm a big fan of the botanical gardens in my hometown. Nature is your friend.
- Practice deep breathing.
- Enjoy kava or a variety of teas.
- Use lavender essential oil. Put just a few drops on your palms, rub together, cup your nose, and inhale deeply. *Immediate relief!*
- Soak in a hot bath. I used to hide in the tub and drink my wine, thinking that was self-care . . . sans the vino now, I do realize a bath bomb or some Epsom salts will help me to sleep better.
- Focus on one thing at a time. Seriously, most of us try to calm down by doing ten things at once. Pick just one thing and try to do it for thirty minutes. Bake, paint your nails, write a note to a friend.
- Try pigeon pose or any other hip-opening exercises that allow you to release held emotions. If you're feeling stressed or angry, this could provide the instant relief you're needing.
- Connect with your people. The power of connection and being heard diffuses negative emotions. Find a friend who won't pile on her shared anger but instead

allows yours to dissipate. (Note: this rarely happens over a few glasses of wine.)

- Write in your journal. This is one of my faves. Once I write it down, I may not even need to vent it out loud.
- Do some cardio with a great playlist. Literally, burn through that negative energy and fuel those endorphins!
- Listen to music. Feeling sad or lonely? Hey, personally, I'm a big fan of worship music, and I've found it's hard to entertain fear and negative emotions when I'm focusing on the God of the universe who is well acquainted with our suffering and sorrow!
- Turn on some inspirational podcasts or videos. I love anything that changes my perspective when I'm feeling stuck!
- Savor some chocolate. Yep! It's okay to go get ice cream with your hubby or friends instead of meeting for the customary drink "to connect."

When you remove alcohol from your life, replace it with something better.

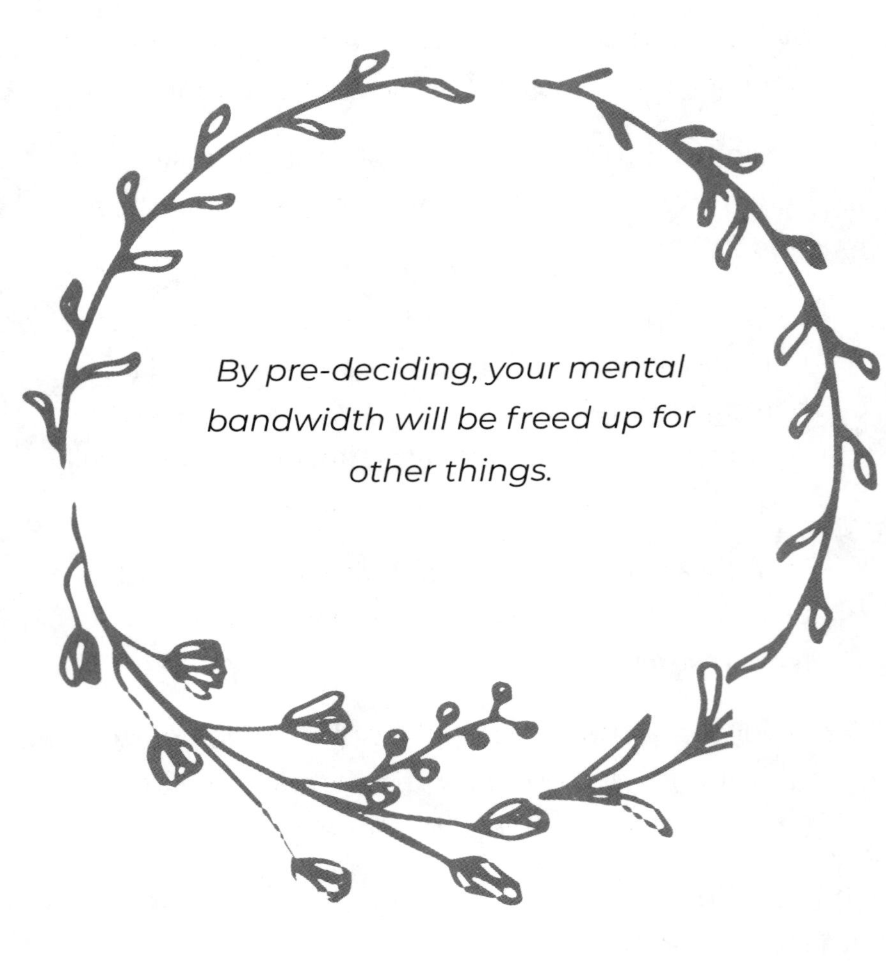

By pre-deciding, your mental bandwidth will be freed up for other things.

Decision Fatigue

Did you know there's actually something called "decision fatigue"? Simply put, you can get tired of choosing. And always weighing alternatives and gathering the energy to do the "right" thing can be particularly exhausting.

Let's say that you are weighing whether or not you want to pour that first glass of wine when you get home from work. You may even feel a tugging inside you as you weigh your options. It's that tug-of-war between the proverbial cartoon angel and cartoon devil.

> Devil: "It has been a rough day, girl! You deserve this."
> Angel: "Sis, you know it's going to feel good for a minute, but you'll regret it in the morning. You've seen this movie before."
> Devil: "But if you can just chill out a little bit, everything will be better."
> Angel: "Will it? Will it really?"

We have this inner battle between what we *should* do and what we *want* to do—and usually end up doing! The

way we're wired, if we haven't made a commitment to do otherwise, we're likely going to choose the path of least resistance.

Exhausting!

It's one of the reasons that whether we're trying to be thoughtful about our choices around alcohol, food, or other little pleasures, many of us have success in the morning hours. We're more likely to stick to our goals early in the day. Each new morning is a fresh start, and intentions are good and strong! But as the hours go on throughout our busy lives, we're making endless minor decisions all day long—What am I making for dinner? Pick up vino at the store? Wait until the clock hits 5 p.m. for the first sip? Maybe stop at *two* tonight?—and that can be fatiguing to our decision-making muscle.

My choice to be alcohol-free means that after I made the single decision not to consume alcohol, I was suddenly *spared* a thousand other smaller decisions throughout the day. If that sounds like freedom, it absolutely is.

Here's my confession: I have the ability to overthink *anything*. (My hubby will vouch for this.) It's sort of like my modus operandi. And it certainly applies to my relationship with drinking. Often, by wine o'clock, I'd have been volleying the decision of whether or not to drink back and forth in my mind like a ping-pong match!

The big win, my friend, is to pre-decide: before the vacation, before the special event, before the date night. Pre-decide what you will or will not drink. Specifically, the formula that has worked for me has been:

1. Pre-decide.
2. Commit.
3. Follow through.

When you take that decision off the table, by pre-deciding, your mental bandwidth will be freed up for other things. And that feels so freeing!

If we examine our beliefs and then consciously choose the ones that are true, the false ones lose their power to bully us.

Rejecting the Lies

The wedding band is playing "Dancing Queen," and I'm practically running to get on the dance floor. I mean, I am getting my groove on. The other guests would have naturally assumed I'd tossed a few back. I was a *young* mom, just happy to be out with other adults! I was full of energy and stayed until the bride and groom left in their fancy car. Life was pretty good.

But here's the thing: *I wasn't yet a drinker.*

Ten years later, I'm actually at the second wedding of the same bride. But now I'm a drinker, though not an experienced one. So, I didn't realize how much Deep Eddy grapefruit vodka would slowly but surely hit me. It tasted like lemonade, and everyone seemed to be enjoying it together. After several hours, it hit me. Like a ton of bricks. And the following morning, it felt like two tons of bricks. But I only had to spend eleven hours in the car that day driving home with a brutal hangover. (Isn't drinking so fun?) The worst part was that my oldest child had observed how affected I'd been by the alcohol the evening before. I was even borderline confused at how sneaky the "I'm fine, no I'm not" shift happened. I certainly wasn't proud. Have you been there?

I had believed a lie: "Drinking enhances an experience." While no one had spoken it explicitly, the savvy marketers of all things alcohol had communicated it to me quite clearly. But *it's just not true*. And I had been bullied by that lie.

Some of us are being bossed around by our beliefs. And for us to take control back in our lives, we need to look at what those beliefs are. When we look at them, we then have the power to decide if the belief to which we're clinging is a lie or if it's true.

- "After this chaotic crisis, I need a drink. Honestly, *anyone* would."
- "This is how adults deal with life in the evenings."
- "I work hard, and I deserve this reward."
- "This is how people unplug."
- "I give so much to everyone else. This is my 'me time.'"
- "This is how people deal with anxiety. It's actually God's *gift* to us. (So, thank you, Jesus.)"
- "Alcohol is vital to my social life."

What I'd believed was that drinking enhances an experience. But I'd never paused to ask myself whether or not my belief was true. Our minds are incredibly powerful, and if we believe we're having more fun because of alcohol, then we probably are. But the flip side is also true: if we believe that alcohol actually doesn't enhance our lives, we'll have more fun without it.

If we examine our beliefs and then consciously choose the ones that are true, the false ones lose their power to bully us. So begin to pay attention to your beliefs. Some will be loud and shouty, and others will be more subtle. Spend some time journaling and try to uncover those tapes that are playing on repeat in your head. Write down everything you've believed about alcohol, about drinking, about drinking while socializing, and about yourself.

Yeah, it's a big assignment, but it's worth it. *You're* worth it.

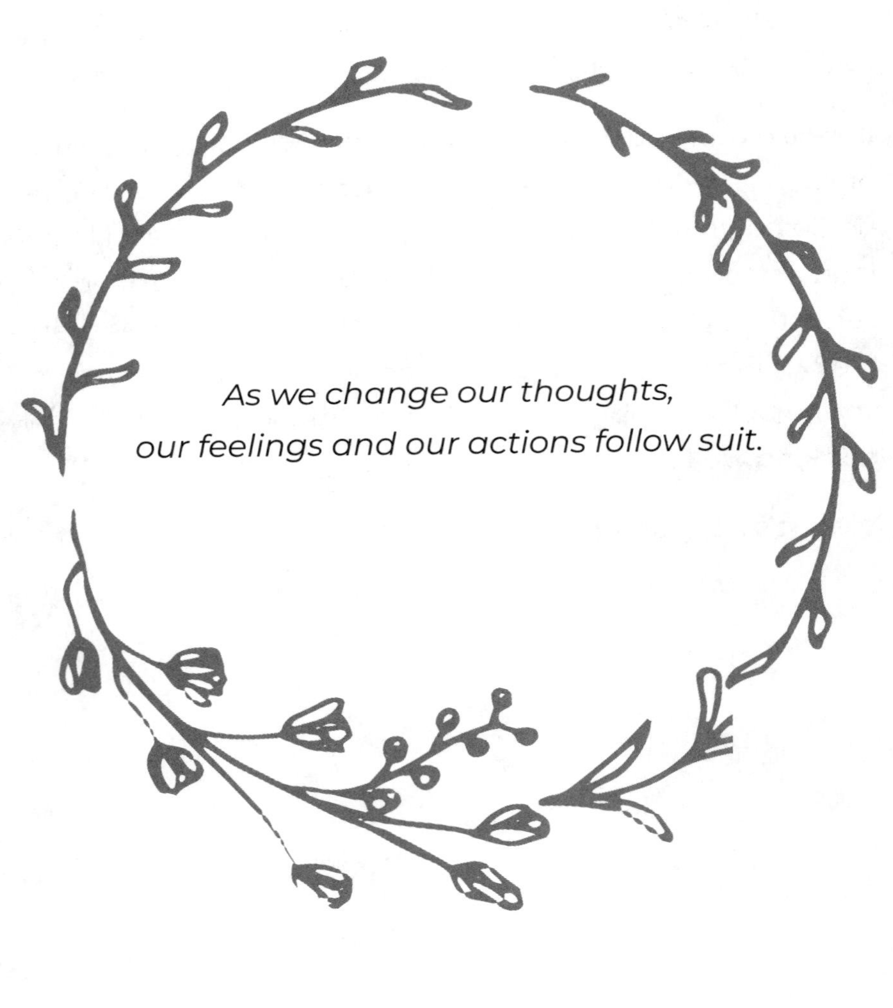

*As we change our thoughts,
our feelings and our actions follow suit.*

Choosing Your Thoughts

I'm going to go out on a limb here and take a guess at something I think is true of you. I'm guessing that you've never had a drink of alcohol without first having the thought, "I want a drink."

Am I right?

Our thinking determines what we feel, and it also determines what we do.

And I want you to hear that while that cycle can keep us trapped in the detox-to-retox loop, it is also exactly what can set us free. While there are thoughts that do bubble up from a deep place in us, as we train ourselves to notice what we're thinking, we're empowered. We get to *choose* our thoughts.

We can choose our thoughts about difficult relationships.

We can choose our thoughts about how we're aging and how we view those wrinkles!

We can choose our thoughts about what we experienced in childhood.

We can choose our thoughts about alcohol.

It's true. You can.

Even if you have practiced thinking the same thoughts for a very, very long time (and rutted a mental pathway), change is still possible.

In fact, the Apostle Paul wrote, "We demolish arguments and every pretension that sets itself up against the knowledge of God, and we take captive every thought to make it obedient to Christ" (2 Corinthians 10:5, NIV). Can you see that in your mind's eye? When we've got these rogue thoughts bouncing around in our heads, flitting about like butterflies, we do not have to be bullied by them. We can capture them—in a glass, in a net—so that they no longer have free rein. In fact Dr. Caroline Leaf, a well-known Christian neuroscientist, studied this phenomenon and shared that actual brain scans show how choosing what we think actually renews our minds! It's real, y'all. It's *science*.

When we fail to take our thoughts captive, we operate from what some call our "flesh," our "lower brain," or our "monkey mind." And in case it's not clear, we do not want a monkey in the driver's seat. But that's exactly what happens when we don't pause to consider what we're thinking.

Some thoughts that just pop into our heads are worth releasing.

"I *need* this drink."

"I *deserve* a treat."

"I *can't live* without this."

Here's the thing, Sis: we have the choice to notice those thoughts and replace them with a thought that's truer than the first twisty thought that came to our minds.

"I *want* this drink, but I don't need it."

"I would very much *like* a treat, but I deserve to treat my body and mind with care and respect."

"I actually *can* live without this."

You see it, right? It's not rocket science. But it is powerful! As we change our thoughts, our feelings and our actions follow suit.

Be the boss of you and choose the thoughts you allow to take up real estate in your head.

Willingness is greater than willpower.

Willingness

You know that poster with the cute fuzzy kitten hanging from a tree? The inspirational slogan emblazoned across the desperate kitty reads, "Hang in There."

While it's absolutely darling in kitten form, I want you to imagine that it's you hanging from the tree limb. You're forty feet in the air (for whatever reason), and you're hanging on for dear life. You're using all of your strength, and the death grip you have on the tree branch is starting to wear thin.

When it comes to alcohol, and specifically problem drinking, we use the phrase "white-knuckling it" to mean that we're alone with no help. We're depending solely on willpower to keep us from drinking.

The next question I hope you're asking yourself is, "So how's that working out for ya?" Because while it can sound sort of badass, it's really not the best strategy. Just as there are uncontrollable variables that throw a wrench into practicing moderation—getting bad news, a stressful

family situation, loss of a job, etc.—the same is true when we decide to use willpower to stop drinking. We might be able to hang from that tree for a while, but eventually there's going to be a gust of wind, a curious raccoon, or a lightning storm that will *test* our white-knuckled willpower.

We need more than willpower.

When we face obstacles—"when," not "if"—we are better served with a posture of "willingness" over "willpower." The cravings we experience are strong. And when we try to deny or ignore the feelings we have, they only get stronger. Maybe you've heard the phrase "What we resist persists."

Willingness says, "This, too, shall pass."

Willingness says, "I want something even better than this immediate gratification."

Willingness says, "I'm willing to break away from the herd and live a life of *real* freedom."

Willingness says, "I'm willing to give up control."

While the *idea* of using willpower does have that strong fierce vibe, ultimately it's not enough.

We need other people.

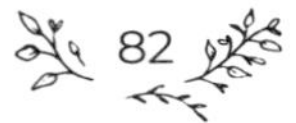

We need tools in our tool belts.

We need sustenance for the journey.

If you're that cat dangling from a tree, willpower *will* work. For a short time. But then your muscles will tire. You'll lose your grip. You'll be blown by the wind. And you'll need a lot more than an inspirational slogan.

Willingness means that you keep showing up for yourself.

Willingness means that you can allow things to be messy, and keep moving forward.

Willingness is being open. You may not have all the answers, but you're willing to keep trying.

I know a lot of women who can white-knuckle it for days or weeks. They succeed, for a time, by sheer willpower. But then a circumstance hits them harder than expected, and willpower fails. This is the story of a number of women in our community. And we're delighted to welcome them into a community where we've learned, together, what works. Willingness is greater than willpower.

We believe that a mindset of making "progress"—by learning, by brushing ourselves off and continuing—is more helpful than a mindset that requires "perfection."

Progress Over Perfection

Mandy had been alcohol-free for fifteen months when, one evening, she had a pretty intense conflict with her teenage daughter. (Can I get a witness, moms?) Feel free to imagine whatever awful, stressful disagreement would make *you* want to turn to alcohol for relief.

After they both stormed off in separate directions, a thought floated into Mandy's mind.

"I'll just have one glass."

At that moment it seemed like the most sane, rational choice in the world.

Pulling the cork, smelling the familiar, soothing aroma wafting from the bottle, Mandy poured her favorite red wine. Slipping the bottle into the back of the utility closet, Mandy dipped into her bedroom for privacy. Lounging on her bed, sipping what felt like liquid calm, everything seemed right with the world.

Until it didn't.

About fifteen minutes later, Mandy's daughter stormed into her bedroom. The sudden entry left Mandy no time to hide her glass.

As she noticed her mother holding the almost empty glass of wine, the look of disgust and disappointment on her girl's face said everything.

What fell from her daughter's lips were the words, "Is this how we handle problems?"

She'd said the exact words that every gray-area drinkin' mama fears. *Am I right?* We don't want to communicate to our kids that alcohol will solve life's problems. And yet in that moment, Mandy's perceptive daughter hit the nail on the head.

The outcome of that awful evening could have gone a couple of ways. Mandy might have doubled down on why having *one* glass of wine (but really, who are we kidding?) was no big deal. Or she might have decided that since she'd already blown it, she might as well just finish the bottle. And another the next night. And the next. (Since she'd fallen off the wagon.) But that's not how it ended.

The look on Mandy's daughter's face, one she never wanted to see again, was enough to snap her out of it.

If we give up when we slip up, then we're harming ourselves and the people we love.

Imagine you're running a marathon and you stumble and fall on mile seventeen. Do you get up, brush yourself off, and go back to the starting line? Or do you get back up and keep running forward? (Even non-runners can figure this one out.) Well, Sis, the alcohol-free race some of us are running together is a marathon, not a sprint. And so, if we're experimenting with the 21 Day Reset, when we stumble on Day 17, we don't throw in the towel. And we also don't have to go back to Day 1.

We. Keep. Going.

We're convinced that we can learn from the feedback our failures provide. We believe that a mindset of making "progress"—by learning, by brushing ourselves off and continuing—is more helpful than a mindset that requires "perfection."

Today Mandy has been alcohol-free for three years, with just that one slipup. She didn't have to start over. She learned from the exchange she had with her daughter, and she kept going. Instead of a setback, it was *valuable* feedback letting her know what was really important.

Friend, you *might* stumble in your alcohol-free living. And you also might fall on your face and be splayed all over the ground. And you can choose to learn from that moment and *keep going.*

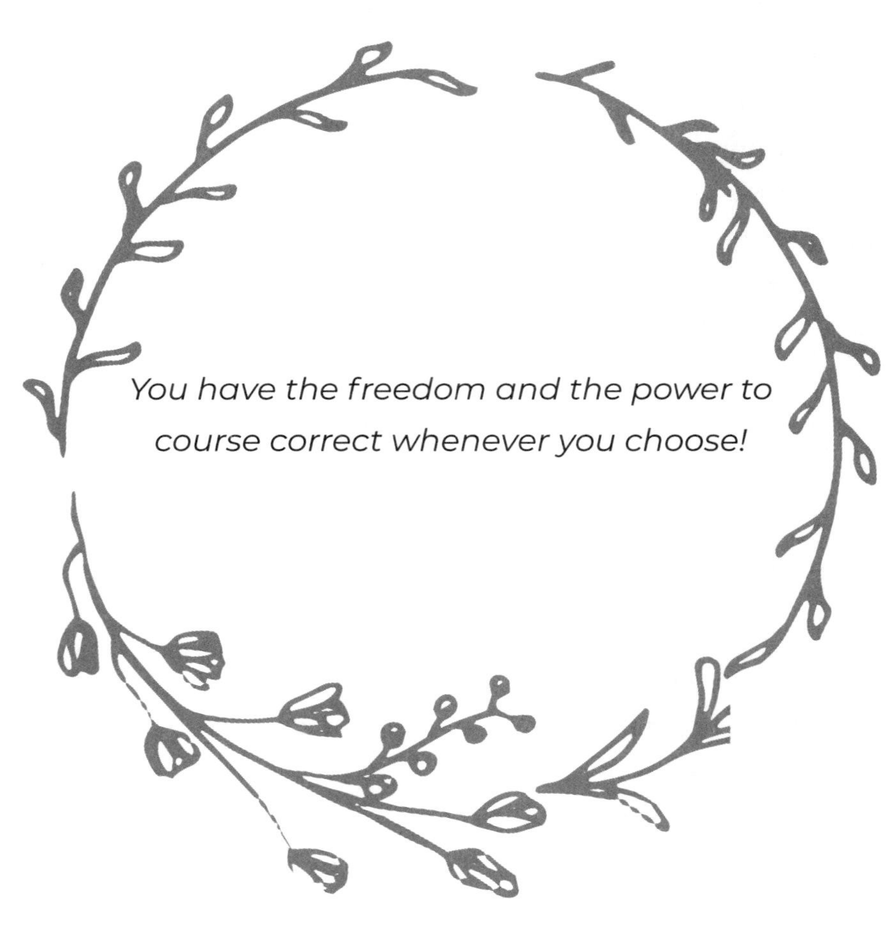

You have the freedom and the power to course correct whenever you choose!

Course Correction

No one wants to wake up Monday morning in reaction mode.

So on Sunday nights I like to pull out my calendar and do a little prep for the week. When I can get a peek at what's coming, I feel way less overwhelmed than when the week's events are barreling at me full speed. Strategies like time blocking, setting realistic goals, and scheduling daily self-care practices are just a few tricks that help me to thrive.

Does everything consistently unfold per my carefully planned schedule? No, it does not. But with a plan I can pad a little bit of room for those unexpected deviations while also having space for course correction. Some people refer to this as "having margin."

Let's say you're sitting at a fundraising dinner, and you showed up with the plan not to drink alcohol. Bravo. But as the featured speaker drones on, you find yourself noticing your neighbor's drink. And smelling your neighbor's drink.

And thinking about your neighbor's drink. And the next thing you know, you're imagining slipping out of your seat, walking to the bar, and returning to your seat with . . . that's right . . . *a drink*.

But I want you to know that you have the power to course correct at any time—especially in your mind before you take action. I've found the battlefield is in the mind!

When you catch yourself fixating on all of the alcoholic drinks around your table or you're starting to rationalize or romanticize drinking, you can choose to think about something else. *Anything* else. You can practice being present in the moment and check in with how your body feels. You can even use my favorite mindset tool: play the movie forward. How do you want to feel later?

When you stand up to visit the bar, you can course correct. You can pivot and ask for sparkling mineral water with lime. You can visit the ladies' room. You can even release some of that energy by climbing hotel stairs. Seriously, you have options!

You have the freedom and the power to course correct whenever you choose! Is the mental pathway around alcohol pretty firmly carved in your brain? It may be. But you can interrupt the process at any time and course correct. The key is sticking with your awareness and not handing over the control of your mind to alcohol. You can actually rewire your brain; it just takes time . . . and practice. The scientific term is *neuroplasticity*, and it works.

"Well, not after I've tasted the first sip, Jenn . . ."

Actually, you even have the freedom to course correct by going so far as to pour it out or switch to water on the next drink! (Is your mind blown right now? I know, I know.)

Sis, whether you're stuck in your thought world or whether you're three sheets to the wind, you always have the choice to shift direction and course correct. Even if you wake up with a splitting headache, that is a moment when you can return to your sober mind and begin choosing different thoughts that lead to different choices. You can do this.

The choice is yours.

We can frame our missteps and slipups as "feedback."

Valuable Feedback

Tina had been living alcohol-free for eight months when she traveled to attend her sister's wedding. She was living in Arizona, and the wedding was in the small Indiana town where the girls had been raised.

Tina's job had been extra stressful the previous week, and because she was scrambling to get out of town, she hadn't paused to make a plan for how she'd navigate staying alcohol-free at the wedding. She hadn't had a chance to really visualize how she wanted to "show up" for herself or others.

Without a car and tight on time, she didn't have the freedom to grab alcohol-free beverages to take to the reception.

She was also walking into a stressful family event. Both girls had suffered some major childhood trauma, and it had never been discussed in the family.

And at the last minute her husband, who was traveling for work and always had Tina's back, had flight delays that kept him from making it to the wedding.

Gritting her teeth to make it through the ceremony without getting emotional, then dodging some of the trickier family members as she dashed to the reception in another wing of the venue, Tina was the first person in line at the open bar.

When she woke up the next morning after a restless night of sleep, beside her husband who'd slipped in late at night, her head was throbbing.

"Babe," she said to her husband, who'd already placed a cup of coffee beside her, "I feel like such a failure. I drank last night."

While there were a lot of *wrong* things he could have said, he'd learned what Tina had discovered during her eight months with Sober Sis, and he offered, "What if you didn't look at it as a failure but rather a valuable experience?"

Tina knew where he was headed.

"What if you thought of this as *feedback* rather than a setback?"

Tina's face brightened a bit.

"Is the feedback the insight that I'm a failure?" she asked playfully.

"Nope," he assured her. "The feedback might be noticing

that you didn't have anything to eat yesterday when you arrived at the wedding."

"True," Tina mused.

"That's something you can change next time. Or," he continued, "feedback might be remembering that *our* wedding was incredibly hard with your family, and this was another difficult emotional environment to be in."

Together they continued to notice and learn from the previous day and days, focusing on the kinds of adjustments Tina could make in the future.

When we frame our missteps and slipups as "setbacks," they *set us back*. Discouraged, set back, we're more likely to drink again. But there's another possibility. We can frame our missteps and slipups as "feedback." Then we not only learn from our experiences, but they can actually propel us forward with more robust resources in our tool belts.

When we "restart the clock" after a setback, setting our alcohol-free time clock back to zero, or "zero days of sobriety," then failures *are* a setback. But we can choose, instead, to keep the clock running and still be honest about the twists and turns our path has taken.

Today Tina is four years living mostly alcohol-free, with that one *really helpful* learning experience along the way.

When we pursue rest, soul rest,
we are restored.

Restorative Rest

This past weekend was awesome. I got a good long walk in on Saturday morning that made me feel *fully alive*. I reread one of my favorite books, *Practicing the Presence of People*. When faced with hard news, I had a good cry. (Did you even know that cries *could* be good? They can. They really can.) And I also got to spend several beautiful quiet hours with God, strolling through my local botanical gardens. The sun caressed my face, and the gentle breeze kept me cool. What I experienced this weekend was genuine, wholehearted *rest*.

What's *not* genuine rest is taking a road trip with a pounding headache because you're completely drained after a night of drinking.

What's *not* genuine rest is a quick nap because your sleep has been so disrupted by alcohol.

What's *not* genuine rest is reaching for a drink to take the edge off.

These easy soothers may provide a little relief, but we were made for so much more.

Priscilla Shirer, founder of Going Beyond Ministries, said, "Pressure. We all feel it. Pressure to keep up. Pressure to keep going. Pressure to stay ahead, stay afloat, stay relevant" (Priscilla Shirer, *Fervent.* Nashville: B&H Books, 2016). The fact is, we're going to feel pressure and get tired. And when we get tired, it's tempting to quit. We can easily slip into a mindset where we abandon our good intentions . . . the "shoulds." It's tempting to reach for what we know will soothe our frayed nerves. But what we need most is genuine rest.

Many times in the past, I would be looking for relief from a long day and looking forward to my glass(es) of wine. Mindlessly sippin' on Pinot Grigio always provided temporary relief by slowing my racing mind but never provided me the deep rest in my soul that I was looking for. This is less about the wine and more about what I was searching for. For me, drinking in the evenings was a distraction, a Band-Aid, and it did offer *temporary* relief from the pressure, the anxiety, or even the boredom—only to have everything come back double when the effects wore off.

We can experience genuine rest, but it requires intention.

We experience genuine rest when we don't just hope for it, but we actually plan for it, writing it into our schedules.

We experience genuine rest when we choose to prioritize a self-care practice and establish healthy boundaries.

And I promise you, the kinds of conflicts that are going to arise when you commit to rest are going to be enticing. Anything in life worth having is likely to invite opposition and resistance. So, if you've blocked out time for "rest" on your calendar—whether spending time in nature or cuddled up in a cozy blanket near a fire—expect resistance. Chances are good that you'll get competing invitations trying to lure you into a life of busyness, the kind of chaotic "running around" that takes you nowhere and leaves you feeling more exhausted.

Sis, you've likely heard me say it before: the race we're running is a marathon, not a sprint. And that's why we commit ourselves to what it takes to succeed over the long haul. We care for our bodies, treating them with respect. We fill our minds with what feeds and strengthens them. We do the necessary emotional work of feeling the feels and creating opportunities for stillness. We tend to and nurture our spirits.

When we pursue rest, soul rest, we are restored.

The truth is, change is going to cost you something.

Committing to Change

"There's no way I'm drinking tonight!"

For years, I *wanted* to not be bossed around by alcohol. I'd wake up in the morning with the very best intentions, wanting change. But by five o'clock I'd have lost track of my "why," that thing that would motivate me to stick to my guns.

When I decided to break out of the detox-to-retox loop, I committed to a six-week break. I made a short-term goal because I needed practice. While I believed in moderation, *in theory*, it hadn't worked for me. Desperate, I decided I was willing to be uncomfortable as I tried something new.

The fact was that I'd *wanted* change for several years. But wanting is passive; it's inactive. I doubt there was one day, over those years, when I wasn't pulled between my two minds: I don't want to drink, I want to drink. (Guess which of those two *wantings* won out, day after day?) Sis, I do not have to tell you, the mental tug-of-war is real. But *wanting* things to change hadn't been enough to create any results. In fact, it left me more frustrated and defeated—creating even more *wanting*. I wanted to *want* to stop drinking. I knew it wasn't serving me. And a part of me even knew that it was holding me back. It wasn't until that *wanting* became a real commitment that I began to see real results.

Sometimes a short-term goal feels more doable, and significantly less intimidating. You can do anything for six short weeks. What are you going to do instead of reaching for a drink?

You can splurge on your favorite bath bombs.

You can go for a long walk.

You can eat a piece of chocolate cake.

My motto the first few weeks was "Jenn, just don't drink, no matter what." And it became about what I *could* focus on doing that was aligning to my goal.

It didn't matter what I did, as long as I stayed away from drinking alcohol. I was laser-focused on a commitment I had made to myself. I was doing this for me. At times it felt lonely, but deep down I had faith that something better was on the other side of this temporary discomfort. I was sick and tired of being sick and tired. And *that*—being sick and tired—was part of my "why"! It was one of the reasons that motivated me to keep going.

And those small, consistent daily choices started to build confidence and momentum as new experiences showed me that I could do it! As I gathered successes—and began feeling so much better physically and emotionally—it became less about "pushing through" and began to feel more like partnering with God on this. I was learning how to live with a new mindset where I didn't feel miserable but instead felt empowered.

The truth is, change is going to cost you something. You've got to be willing to sacrifice something you have for something you want. It's going to be uncomfortable. It's going to be disruptive. It will disrupt the status quo. And it is *so* worth it.

If you're like me, you've wanted change for a while. But until you commit to it—to doing the work, to being uncomfortable—*wanting* isn't going to get you where you want to be. And you *can* get there, Sis! It's a matter of committing to it.

If you're growing, you will experience growing pains.

Growing Pains

I was recently on an airplane, and the pilot announced that we'd be encountering some turbulence as we ascended. He saw it coming; he looped us in; we buckled our seat belts. It was fairly bumpy as we climbed through the sky. But when we finally hovered above the clouds, at 40,000 feet, it became a relatively smooth ride.

Are you experiencing a bumpy ride?

Now, you might be on a bumpy journey because you're experiencing the consequences of your choices. You wake up with a headache more days than not. Your relationships are being affected by your drinking. You're not living the life you want to be living. We've all been there. But that's not the "bumpy" I'm talking about.

I'm talking about the "bumpy" that comes when we're ascending to a new place. When we're growing. When we're being transformed.

If you're growing, then you're likely facing challenges. You might be coming up against some resistance, internally from deep within or from the people around you who are used to you showing up like you have in the past. And you might even be feeling weary or discouraged. Girl, if that's you, I get it. I've been there. (I may even be there *today*.) But I want you to hear that if the growth in your life is making you feel uncomfortable, *you're exactly where you need to be*.

Maybe your bestie isn't supportive of your choice to put a pause on drinking alcohol. You feel like she's giving you the side-eye about it.

Or maybe your partner is complaining that you're no fun anymore. (*That* says more about your partner than about you.)

Or you might be dreading going home for the holidays and navigating the culture of drinking that pervades your family.

If that's what you're facing, I'm sorry. And I'm also so proud of you. Those kinds of pressures are to be expected when we start making life-giving choices to be the best version of ourselves. Without alcohol, when you show up to be fully present in your life, you're going to feel some of the bumps that were numbed with alcohol.

It's not a question of whether we'll face obstacles. We will. We absolutely will. But what we have control over is how we're going to navigate the bumps.

Will you put on your seat belt and stay the course? Will you keep loving your bestie or your partner when they can't support you? Will you make a plan for that visit home so that you can navigate unexpected detours?

If you're growing, you will experience growing pains. It comes with the territory. And you are choosing to be brave by entering uncharted territory as you begin to—or continue to—navigate the alcohol-free life.

Sis, I believe that you've got everything you need for this journey. So whatever storms of life you're encountering today, I encourage you to buckle up, go through the turbulence, and keep the faith knowing that smooth, sunny skies are ahead. Keep going and growing, the best is yet to come. Remember, you're not where you used to be! Onward and upward!

When you face uncomfortable feelings, receive them as the gift they are.

An Unexpected Gift

After a hard conversation with a friend recently, my feelings got hurt. When I was washing dishes later that evening, I noticed that my insides were still stinging.

Can you relate? Because I'll bet you've been in this place of emotional dysregulation, too.

Maybe getting ghosted by a guy triggered an old wound of rejection inside you.

Or the bad behavior of a family member has you so angry that you want to set something on fire.

Or maybe financial obligations have piled up, and you're really scared about how you'll be able to meet them.

Or you might be feeling ashamed of a certain way you behaved.

When our feelers are activated, when we feel that "edge," we're more vulnerable to making decisions we'll regret. We're tempted to soothe those hard feelings, to numb ourselves, when we feel that edge.

When I was drinking, I knew how the "hurt feelings" movie would have ended. I'd be a little taken aback by my friend's bluntness. I'd stew on it for a while, simmering inside. Then I'd comfort myself with a glass or two of wine. (But really, who's counting?)

Today, though, rather than finding *new* ways to take the edge off, I'm choosing to pay attention to it. To learn from what it wants to teach me.

So, after this recent conversation that had really bruised my heart, I allowed myself to cry. (Pro tip: the only way beyond the feels is to go *through* the feels.) Then I grabbed my journal and let myself process what had happened. Using the written word as a tool, I recounted the incident and reflected on why it had felt so sharp.

And what's different, today, about paying attention to that sharp edge rather than dulling it, is that I was able to be curious about why I received her words the way I did and how I even spoke up, being honest with my friend. Trust me, if the thought of potential conflict overwhelms you, you're not alone. It feels brave and like a necessity to my emotional health to keep "short accounts" with those important to me. I don't want resentments to build up . . . that dulls my edge, *too*. Good news, I moved through it and was not emotionally incapacitated the next day. What used to knock me down and take me out of the game no longer did. I wasn't erased. I didn't check out. It hurt me, *because I am human*, but it didn't destroy me.

In fact, I've even found that I *need* that edge. It gives me valuable feedback that helps me to make the best choices. When we allow the edge to teach us rather than dulling it, we choose to stay sober-minded. We choose to be alert, aware, and awake in our own lives. And we need that sober mind for clarity, feedback, and direction. When we opt to be sober-minded, we choose to stay sharp.

Precious Sis, let your *edge* be a gift. When you face uncomfortable feelings, receive them as the gift they are. Because that edge is often what we need in order to hear God's whisper through all the chaos. It's what alerts us to the way in which we can receive, grow, and transform.

We can renew our minds by the purposeful choices that we make throughout the day.

Renew Your Mind

My friend, who I'll call Dana, just got back from an annual girls' trip. It was her first one since she made the decision to live alcohol-free, and she was the only one not drinking.

You can likely see how this excursion might be tricky, right? It's easy to imagine that Dana's mind might have been swirling with thoughts before this adventure . . .

"What will they think of me?"

"Will they still think I'm fun?"

"Will *I* still think I'm fun?"

"Will I be tempted?"

"What if I just can't connect with them?"

"What if it's not the same without alcohol?"

It's natural to try to imagine what is going to be different after we stop drinking.

But Dana made a conscious choice before the trip. Rather than focusing on what she might be losing out on by

iving alcohol-free, she decided to focus on what she would be gaining by being sober-minded when she was with her friends.

"I'm going to be more present with these women."

"I'm going to be in a better position to love well and actively listen."

"I'm going to be able to evaluate whether these are friendships I'll continue to pursue."

"I'm going to stay connected to my authentic self."

Knowing that there might be some challenges, Dana had decided to exercise her new healthy boundaries by deciding, for herself, when she showed up and when she left. And she did decide to leave a bit earlier in the evening than some of the others. She even brought some of her favorite alcohol-free canned drinks to the pool at the hotel. It was a great win because her friends who were drinking didn't care either way what beverage was in her hand. It was no big deal. There was no judgment either way, and that felt really good. Dana's decisions about how she thought about her girls' trip is what made it a success for her!

Sis, you can also make choices about what thoughts you allow to take up space in your mind. The truth is that we all have certain thoughts in our heads that play on repeat.

And when we replay the same thoughts again and again, they actually grow *stronger*.

"I need this."

"I deserve this."

"I earned this."

But one thing we can do is set an intention and choose what we will focus on. We can literally "fix our eyes" on things above . . . maybe that's thinking about eternal things, becoming the best version of yourself, or reinforcing the positive intentions you have set. This is one of the reasons why it's so important to start your day with prayer, meditation, and reminding yourself of the things you know to be true. That's just one way to retrain your brain!

Whatever you are facing today, or this week, you have the opportunity to choose how you'll think about it. You can frame and create the narrative of your own story by the way you choose to look at things. We can renew our minds by the purposeful choices that we make throughout the day. And what we set our minds on is going to determine how we feel about a situation.

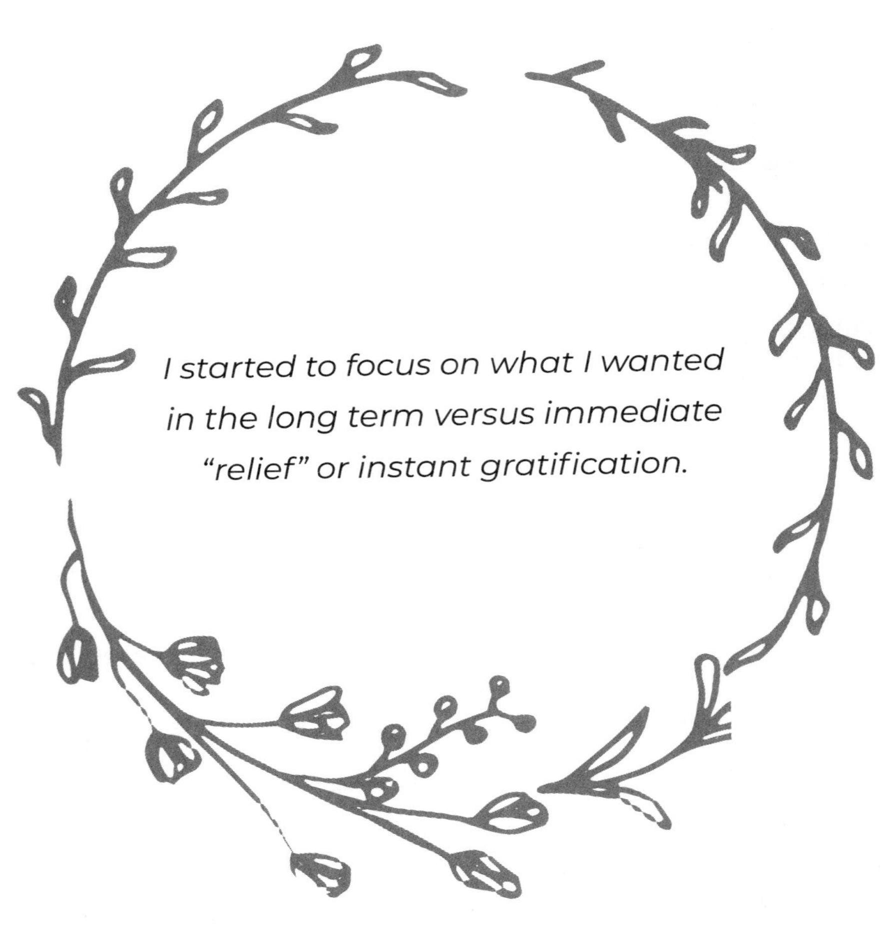

I started to focus on what I wanted in the long term versus immediate "relief" or instant gratification.

Doing Hard Things

Lie: "Numbing out will make everything that is hard *easier* to deal with."

Truth: "Numbing out makes everything hard feel even *worse* and more difficult."

In the past, looking for relief from a long day, I eagerly anticipated my glass(es) of wine. It always provided a temporary reprieve by slowing my mind down, but it never provided the deep rest that I was desperately longing to experience. I honestly thought if I was anxious or worried, that having a drink would help. I didn't yet know the science behind how anxiety and alcohol mix with each other. (Hint: it's kind of like pouring gasoline on a fire!) But everything that I was anxious about and the feelings I was trying to avoid were still there when the numbing effects of the alcohol wore off. In fact, I felt *less* able to deal because I then had a foggy mind.

I've learned from Brené Brown that we can't *selectively* numb. When I was anesthetizing my negative emotions

I wanted to escape, I was numbing sadness *and* joy. I feeling less anxious, but I was also feeling less resilient. Ultimately, I was just experiencing temporary relief. But that actually made things worse. And for a long time, it was hard to make this connection. I gave so much value to my unhealthy relationship with this reality-bending elixir that I was "outsourcing" the job of dealing with what I needed to face to something *outside* of myself when really what I needed was *inside*.

How do you break out of this rut? I started to focus on what I wanted in the long term versus immediate "relief" or instant gratification. The marathon runner who is training to complete the race makes choices like this every day. Run a few miles, or eat a sundae and then take a nap? Only one of those choices is going to serve the long-term goal.

The temptation is understandable, right? When we're hurting, when we're stinging, it's like the solution that lets us exit the pain of our lives—the "eject button"—is just an arm's length away. I've done it, and I speak from experience when I say that it makes what is hard *harder*. It makes what is painful more excruciating. Pouring alcohol on a problem only makes it worse. If you're having a conflict with your spouse, or others in your life, alcohol only fuels the fire! Suspending reality for a moment still

means that you enter back into the pain right where you left off—but even lower than when you made the exit. It keeps you stuck.

Think about when you're grieving or feeling anxious. Did you know that alcohol itself induces *more* anxiety and lower feelings than you had before you started drinking? It seems almost cruel to throw a drink at the pain, driving it into hiding, burying itself deep in the basement. Then the anticipation of dealing with it becomes an added stress. When I was using a drink to ease my mind or soothe my weary heart, I thought I was helping. In reality, I was actually hurting myself more and making matters worse.

Sis, the naughty lie we've believed is that choosing to numb ourselves is going to make things better.

It doesn't.

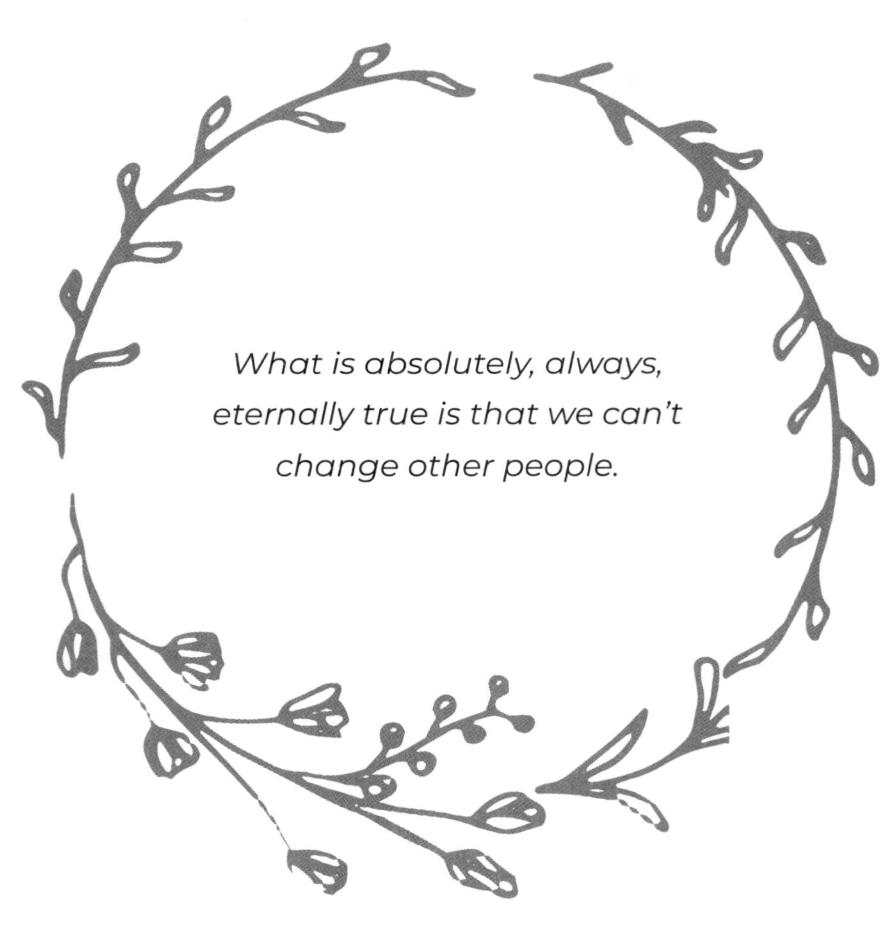

What is absolutely, always, eternally true is that we can't change other people.

Personal Change

"If my teenagers weren't so difficult, I wouldn't need this drink."

"If my husband could understand me better, I wouldn't have to drink."

"If my boss weren't such a challenge, I wouldn't be obsessed with craving this drink."

"If alcohol weren't so prevalent in our world, I wouldn't feel so pressured!"

Guess what? Every single one of those things may be true. It's also the case that they may not be true. What is absolutely, always, eternally true is that *we can't change other people*.

The place where this issue comes up most often in our Sober Sis community is when women make the choice not to drink and their partner does not. Let's face it: we live in an alcohol-centric society. So if you're considering or embracing the choice to be alcohol-free, you might be asking:

- “What do I do if I feel triggered by his drinking choices?”
- “Won’t I be missing out, since we used to enjoy drinking as a couple?”
- “What should I do if others are disappointed or even frustrated that I’m not drinking?”

If you choose to change your drinking habits, it can have a huge ripple effect on others. Anytime one person changes inside a marriage, it affects the relationship. This can be positive or negative, depending on the change and the way it is framed.

If you and your spouse drank often together, your choice not to drink can be a big change in your relational pattern and social life. For my hubby and I, drinking had been a part of most date nights. We did things like wine tours and beer tastings as a hobby. And I understand how it can be a *hope* that your partner will want to make similar changes with you, but it can’t be an *expectation*.

The fact is, you can’t change other people; you can only change yourself. And that’s why our focus should be on healthy marriage with boundaries and good communication rather than changing someone else.

I married my college sweetheart and my best friend. I have discovered when I *ask* for what I need, he is open to meeting that need if it’s possible for him. Since I’ve chosen

an alcohol-free lifestyle, he continues to drink socially and pop a beer or two after a bike ride or while enjoying evening tinkering in his man cave. We are different in this lifestyle choice as individuals, and that's okay. But when we're trying to intimately connect on every level, like an anniversary dinner or a couple's trip, I feel more connected when we're both of sober mind. I've asked him to consider refraining just during that time, not in an effort to change him but to create better intimacy for both of us. Thankfully, my guy is more than happy to do this for me as an act of love and honor.

I'm going to make it plain: *don't try to make your partner stop drinking.* I know I dislike when someone is trying to "fix" or change me. A judgmental attitude toward your partner, or questioning their drinking, will probably cause defensiveness. But if you have an honest, accepting relationship without judgment, it's *possible* that your choice can offer someone you love needed space to reflect. And this might lead to the intrinsic motivation to change.

The way you narrate your journey is up to you.

Owning Your Story

"Can I get you a drink?"

They were the six words I dreaded.

It felt like a huge spotlight would be shining on my response.

Sometimes they'd be asked by a server or bartender. Or they might fall off the lips of a well-meaning family member at a holiday gathering. Or they might even be innocently spoken by one of my girlfriends, in the earliest days of my journey living alcohol-free. Honestly, people are usually just trying to be the "hostess with the mostest" or at a restaurant doing their job. I was very concerned with what people thought about me. (I hadn't yet discovered that they were likely not even thinking about me.)

At the beginning of my journey, I feared the question because there were so many ways I could answer that were destined to end badly.

"No." (Met by a weird stare.)

"I'm not drinking. But . . . no judgment. If you wanna drink, that is *awesome*. I mean . . . *really great*. I support you wholeheartedly."

"No poison for me today. Did you know it's flammable? No thanks!"

"Umm . . . well . . . actually . . . I'm doing this thing . . . I mean, it's kind of like a challenge . . . and I'm like four days in . . . and . . . I guess . . . the way I heard about it was . . ."

In my mind I only saw a host of awkward moments if I made the decision not to drink. And if you've ever been in that position—or if you're dreading it today—let's keep it real. Because I am convinced that you can take that potentially awkward moment and make it a win. So, let's replay . . .

"Can I get you a drink?"

"Absolutely. I'd love to start with some water. I'm so thirsty."

You see what I did there, right? I'm a big fan of saying yes whenever you can! And you *can*.

You can ask the restaurant's cool bartender to make you a mocktail, an alcohol-free cocktail.

You can choose a fancy sparkling water and add a splash of lime.

While we're used to assuming that every "drink" has alcohol in it—because the word has been assumed to mean alcohol—you can still say yes to a cool liquid refreshment. You can say yes to a drink that doesn't happen to include alcohol.

Honestly, I never set out to become totally alcohol-free (partly because I didn't think I could actually do it). For me, the language used by many in the recovery community—"alcoholic," "addict," "recovery," "relapse"—didn't fit. This isn't an issue of wrong or right but rather a personal perspective, perhaps based on where you see yourself on the drinking spectrum. But when I stepped back from the all-or-nothing thinking, I was able to find what worked for me.

I want you to hear that the way I narrate my journey is up to me. The way you narrate your journey is up to you. So today, if someone has questions about my choices, I'll say something like, "I'm choosing to live an alcohol-free lifestyle, and I value, guard, and protect my sober mind."

It works, right? It really works. You choose whether you will drink or not drink, and you choose how you narrate your choices to others.

*In our alcohol-centric society,
drinking is postured and promoted
as a magical connector when really
it is a disconnector.*

Relationships

It was a Thursday night, and my hubby and I had "date night" on our calendar. It had been a challenging day for both of us. He had to confront someone in the office about their behavior, and I had to walk alongside our thirteen-year-old as he faced real disappointment after not being selected for the basketball team. Both of our experiences that day had been about doing hard things and giving support to others. Now we longed for a deposit back into our own relational bank. As usual, we looked forward to dinner at our favorite spot because of the patio view and, of course, the happy hour drinks. Immediately, we sat down and flagged the server to get his cold beer and my glistening glass of Sauvignon Blanc on the table—stat.

We were both anticipating the "relief" from the day, and I hoped it would subdue my sad heart from earlier and make me more chilled out overall. I told myself, "Relax, Jenn, you don't want to be seen as a weak worrier—or worse, someone to fix!" But my emotions were at the surface. I was also feeling frustrated about a

conversation my hubs and I had a few days ago where I felt misunderstood. But I didn't want to risk conflict on our date night. I tucked in my feelings even though I desperately needed a deep connection with my husband.

Drink one. My nerves calmed within minutes, my anxiety started to lift, and my problems and heartache seemed a little further away. This was like a buffer, and it felt good! Except I was also getting further away from my real feelings and starting to get further away from my authentic self.

Drink two. Riding the wave, keeping the buzz up, but this was unsustainable. I was at a crossroads: go to another place for music and my "dessert drink" or go home? Either way, the connection I longed for was elusive, and I was starting to get emotional as my brain lost access to the control grip it'd had all day. We ended up going home.

I had another glass on the back porch while he had a Jack and Coke in his man cave. We never connected. We ended the night alone with our drinks. Sad, isn't it?

In our alcohol-centric society, drinking is postured and promoted as a magical connector when really it is a disconnector. Instead of people truly moving toward one another, we're actually drifting away from each other's presence. It's seen as a social lubricant and is often our "signal" to start having fun. Ask yourself this question: after

a drink (or three) are you more present or less present in reality? First off, it takes us away from ourselves. Think about it. How can we genuinely connect with others when we're becoming more separated from our true essence? As our brain literally becomes hijacked by alcohol, we get out of our rational side and head over to our lizard brain! At this point, silly arguments happen, emotional meltdowns surprise us, and the memories we are there to make get lost. I don't know about you, but that doesn't sound very connecting to me!

Bottom line, alcohol has a way of causing an invisible distance between two people as they become further under the influence. At best, it's putting on rose-colored glasses and staying on the surface, or at worst, it's saying regretful things you can't take back. Connect with the people in your life by being totally present, awake, alert, and aware in your own life. Look alive, Sis!

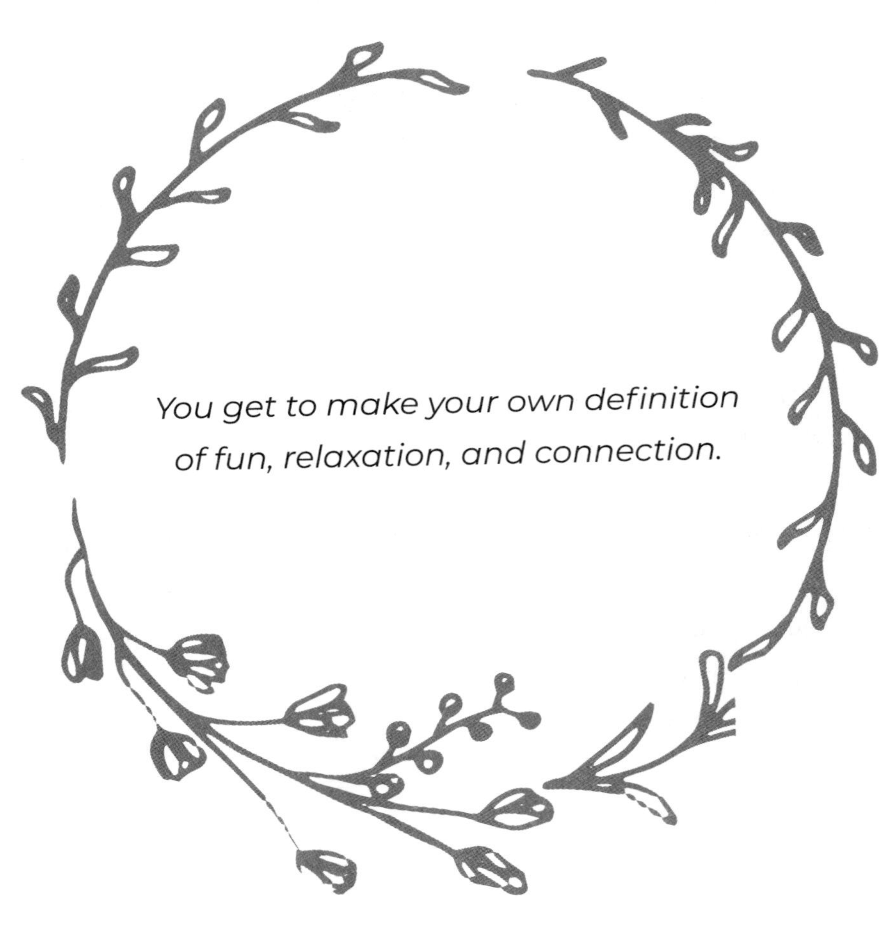

You get to make your own definition of fun, relaxation, and connection.

Alignment

"C'mon, you're not drinking?" Sue's friend demanded.

The women from the office had gathered for their monthly happy hour at a local hot spot known for its strong margaritas.

"Umm . . ." Sue hedged, trying to come up with an excuse for why there wasn't yet a drink in front of her.

Without much conviction, she mumbled, "I probably will . . ."

Waving the bartender over, gesturing toward Sue, her coworker instructed, "She'll have a margarita!"

Whether or not you've stopped to think about it, if you've ever been in a social group that drinks together and have chosen not to drink, you already know this vibe. And the vibe you've noticed is *real*. There is an unwritten social rule that when certain groups gather, there *will* be drinking and the people who show up *will* participate.

Birthday parties. (Even at children's celebrations these days.)

A New Year's Eve bash.

Book club.

Girls Night Out.

For years, I followed society's unspoken rule that said you needed to drink when out at a dinner with friends, on vacation, or at a wedding in order to have fun, relax, or just feel glamorous. I never really questioned why or what was behind this unwritten, and unspoken, social expectation. Instead, I accepted it and played by the rules of our alcohol-centric culture. It's almost as if alcohol were essential and the "guest of honor" at so many gatherings. So I, and a lot of other people, would drink on autopilot in an effort to subdue social anxiety or even to appease others.

Well, guess what!? I'm a bit of a rebel these days because I don't believe that to be true anymore. I created a different "rule" that worked for me. And you also get to make your own definition of fun, relaxation, and connection.

Today I no longer go with the flow, or "go along to get along." Actually, I'm free to do what feels best for me. And you are, too.

What about you? Would you consider yourself a rebel or a rule follower by nature? I put myself in the "rebel" camp because I'm drawn toward understanding the *why* behind the rules. If I think they make sense, I tend to step in line. But I also know which rules are meant to be kept and which ones are okay to break.

If you don't have a lot of "rebel" in you, I want you to know that just because there's an expectation, a social rule, or a shared belief in a group, you are not obliged to follow it! I encourage you to reevaluate a lot of the social beliefs you've accepted by examining the difference between myth and truth. For example . . .

Myth: "Everybody drinks at this event."

Truth: "Many people drink at this event. I am not." (You may be surprised to find that some of your girls weren't drinking when you thought they were!)

Sis, you have the power to make the authentic choice that aligns with the best version of yourself.

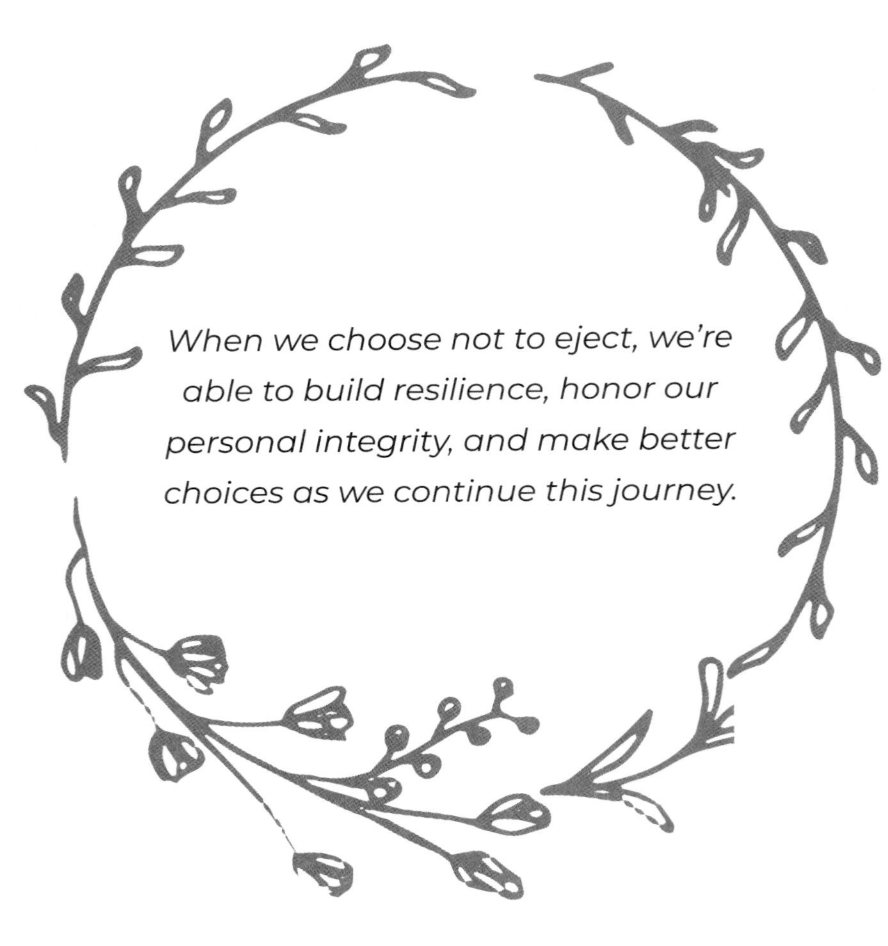

When we choose not to eject, we're able to build resilience, honor our personal integrity, and make better choices as we continue this journey.

Staying Present

Some of us seasoned gals remember what an "eject button" was for. Cassette players, CD players, and DVD players had an eject button for when we wanted to spit the cassette or disc out of the machine. The dangerous *human* version of this is when a fighter pilot, whose jet has failed, ejects himself from his aircraft and opens his parachute to float to the ground.

Those of us who will never fly a fighter jet do use the same technique to extract ourselves from feelings that seem to overwhelm us or cause us to want to bend reality a bit.

We choose "eject" when we bail on our good intentions from early that morning.

We choose "eject" when we soothe a heartache, and avoid our feelings, with a pint of Rocky Road while bingeing Netflix.

We choose "eject" when we pour our drink of choice so that we don't have to feel, don't have to deal.

Sis, please know I've hit that eject button more times than I can count! And I made it out alive, still standing. You know there's no judgment in this space. I know it's hard to sit trapped in a moving car with conflict between others swirling inside, just counting down the minutes till you can order a glass of wine at dinner. In fact, can I tell you something? Sometimes, I "pre-gamed" and had one before we got in the car just to dull my nerves so I wouldn't be so sensitive to it all. I can relate if you've ever had your feelings hurt, been misunderstood, or just felt challenged and looked for an escape hatch . . . because the pain felt like it would crush you. You drank "at" it to make it stop or at least to silence it for a bit. I've even hit the eject button out of sheer boredom and as a way to alter my circumstances. (I thought I was enhancing my presence, but I was just drifting away.)

Today, though, I am making the choice not to use it. Instead, I'm choosing to do hard things. Even when it's uncomfortable, I'm opting to stay in the moment.

Let's say I'm at a dinner party and, as the only person without a cocktail in my hand, I'm feeling left out. Because I'm sober-minded, I'm noticing what's happening in the room and realizing it's not even an atmosphere I'm enjoying. But for a variety of reasons—motivated by love and not by comfort—I stick it out. I stay present in the moment, and as the evening continues, I feel more and more gratitude for staying true to myself.

And guess what I do afterward? I reward myself! (No, the reward is *not* vino.) As I'm going through my bedtime routine, I may plan an early morning walk for the next day. I give myself the treat of waking up at sunrise without a headache, dry mouth, and brain fog. For you, it might be another form of self-care that you want to use as a reward. You might choose a pedicure, a swim in the ocean, or meeting a friend for breakfast.

But I also want you to hear that staying present in the moment has its own rewards! When we're sober-minded, when it's not all about us, we notice when our partner appears to be feeling low. When we choose to stay in the moment, we are able to be fully present to a sister, a friend, a child. When we choose not to eject, we're able to build resilience, honor our personal integrity, and make better choices as we continue this journey.

Choosing to stay present in the moment means that we'll experience discomfort sometimes. But guess what? We can handle that! We can cope with negative reality. There may be a voice whispering in our ear that we will *crumble* or *explode* if we don't pick up a drink, but that's actually untrue.

You got this, girl. You can choose to stay present in the moment.

You are in charge of your thinking.

Being in Charge

One evening my husband and I were at our favorite taco spot, and—like we had always done—he ordered a cold beer. I was just a couple of weeks into my alcohol-free journey, and I was determined not to give in to temptation. But when I tried to order a zero-proof margarita, the server looked at me like I had two heads. At that time there were no alcohol-free options at this particular establishment, except for sugary soda. So as I looked at having a glass of water alongside my tasty tacos, I felt both deprived and defeated. I was experiencing emotional deprivation. I actually went into the restroom and shed a tear behind the safety of the stall door.

When I returned to my right mind, I felt like I'd been a two-year-old throwing an emotional temper tantrum. In that moment, I had given alcohol a very high value *in my thinking*. What I hadn't yet learned is this: I am in charge of my thinking. You are in charge of your thinking.

It took a lot of practice, but the way I changed my deprivation mindset was by changing my perspective in the way I thought about drinking. I started shifting from a place of looking at the negative to choosing to focus on the positive. I know, I know, it sounds corny. But let me explain.

At parties or other get-togethers, I had been afraid of feeling socially awkward or left out. I also feared handling my anxiety or loneliness without a buzz. But that kind of thinking wasn't doing me any favors. So, I started flipping the narrative and thinking about all the things that I was *gaining* by no longer just mindlessly sipping. If you've been on this road for a minute, you can probably tick off your own list. But I'll tell you what was on mine:

- I slept (mostly) through the night. (No 3 a.m. wake-up call!)
- I didn't wake up under a cloud of regret.
- I didn't have a foggy brain in the morning.
- I wasn't pushed around by the hangover effects of alcohol the next day.

My mindset is what was setting me up to experience "deprivation." But when I flipped that mindset on its head, I actually began to be grateful for no more middle-of-the night wake-ups, brutal mornings, and sluggish days. Sis, this was B.I.G. *Big*.

The first step in any change is *awareness*, understanding what you can and cannot control. And you can control how you think about your experience.

Do I still love grabbing tacos at that restaurant with my man? Absolutely. But today I am focused on the *goodness* of missing out on all the negative consequences that came with drinking. Friend, I encourage you to stay mindful. The next time you feel like you're missing out because you're not drinking, look for the endless benefits.

When we're wise enough to make a concrete decision with intention and plan for success, God is our sure and steady helper when temptation comes our way.

Pre-Deciding

On her cross-country flight to L.A. to meet a potential client, Leslie found herself remembering her last trip to the city of angels. She'd been proud of her choice to opt out of in-flight drinks but hadn't really considered the after-dinner "meetup" she'd be attending later in the evening. And although she hadn'*t planned* on drinking, she also hadn't planned on *not* drinking. So, when the bartender came for her order, she went straight to her default response, and the familiar words tumbled right off her lips.

This trip, though, Leslie had tools in her tool belt to help her navigate what was sure to be an alcohol-rich environment. She had *pre-decided* she was not drinking. When we decide in advance not to drink, we avoid those impulsive, reactionary urges that inevitably arise.

Because Leslie had pre-decided not to drink, after her flight landed, she called the restaurant to check to see if they served mocktails. Or if they had any other alcohol-free choices on their menu. They did.

Then, because she had pre-decided not to drink, she arranged her schedule so that she could arrive at the restaurant early and loop in the bartender. (Brilliant!) She preferred to keep her choices on the down-low, to avoid coworkers' inevitable questions about why she wasn't drinking. (It was, after all, about making the best choice *for her*, not making a statement.)

Finding the bartender, she described the group she'd be meeting that evening and gave him his marching orders.

"Frank?" she began, reading his name tag. "Frank, I'd love for you to make me something that's alcohol-free tonight. Something sweet? Something sour? Something spicy? Surprise me!"

Then she dipped out to check her makeup in the bathroom before meeting her crew.

Leslie succeeded that night because she had *pre-decided*. And by pre-deciding, she eliminated "maybe" fatigue and was able to dial in to her clients and make a personal connection.

Psalm 20:4 echoes this time-tested wisdom: "May He grant you according to your heart's desire, and fulfill all your plans." Does God help us when we're flying by the seat of our pants? Sure. But He also gives us wisdom. When we're wise enough to make a concrete decision with intention and plan for success, God is our sure and steady helper when temptation comes our way. Which it inevitably *will*.

If you haven't made a decision ahead of time, more than likely you'll find yourself where Leslie did on her first trip. Probably with a drink in your hand, again. And if you don't pre-decide and instead choose to "play it by ear," the chances are high that your "maybe" will turn into a "yes" for drinking.

So how do you plan to pre-decide when it comes to your next encounter with a group that is drinking?

Maybe you'll duck into the venue early and chat it up with the bartender.

After your server introduces herself to your table, you might excuse yourself to go to the restroom and ask her what zero-proof cocktails are available.

If you're going on vacation with the in-laws, bring your own alcohol-free choices to have on hand.

If you've been invited to the home of a good friend—who may not be alcohol-free but wants to support your journey—you can drop off your own alcohol-free beverages the afternoon of the dinner party for her to serve you that night!

Sis, you do yourself a favor—and eliminate the fatigue of "maybe"—when you pre-decide.

Choose JOMO over FOMO.

Choosing Joy

When you're scrolling through social networking sites, you kind of know how it goes.

"Wait, the two of them went to the beach this weekend? Why didn't they invite me?"

"Another picture-perfect family photo. I wish mine were that way."

"She posted a picture from this party she was at tonight, and—even though I wouldn't really have wanted to be there—I wish I'd been invited!"

"It looks like they had so much fun at the game together."

In the curated feed where we only post pictures of ourselves living our best lives, it's easy to succumb to FOMO.

The term *FOMO*—the fear of missing out—was introduced in the early 2000s, naming the way that seeing everyone's lives on social sites can make us feel like we're missing out.

It's real, right? I have friends who hate going to parties, but if they see a post of their friends at one, they get all bummed that they're missing out on something they didn't want to do in the first place. (It's crazy, right?)

The same phenomena can happen when we make the choice not to drink alcohol. If we've believed that alcohol is the magical potion that makes us super fun and attractive at parties (but, really, does it?), then we may feel anxious and fearful about how to navigate certain social spaces without it.

But guess what? The choice about how you're going to think about your evening when you are around those. who are drinking, the way you *frame* it, is up to you. Could you choose to laser-focus your attention on what you're missing out on? Sure. And many do. But I want to encourage you to make a different choice. Choose JOMO over FOMO.

Choose *joy*!

Now before you write me off as some kind of perky lunatic, I want you to know that focusing on the joy of missing out has been a great tool for *many* in our Sober Sis community. Try thinking of choosing JOMO as a practice of gratitude. So here's what it might look like . . .

When the first round of drinks comes, you can be grateful that you're there with your people.

As you confidently sip your zero-proof cocktail, you can be grateful that you no longer have to drink to feel calm.

As you notice that you're able to drive home safely, sleep soundly, and wake up feeling refreshed the next day, you can be grateful for freedom.

You experience the joy of missing out when you're able to give thanks for all of the beautiful benefits that you're receiving from alcohol-free living. You choose to be grateful that your relationships have improved. You choose to be grateful that you have more money in your pocket to spend on the things that matter most to you. You choose to be grateful that you have the ability to feel all of your feelings and you no longer need to check out to avoid them.

In every moment you have the freedom *to choose joy and gratitude.*

Self-care is not selfish.

Self-Care

I've run my bath and dropped in a bath bomb. For bath bomb newbies, these little "gifts" create beautiful bubbles and make for a pampering experience! Girl, I ain't gonna lie: *this is my happy place!* And tonight I'm treating myself to this luxurious pleasure because I made it through a high school reunion alcohol-free. (I hear your thunderous applause, Sis. Thank you. It's big, right?!)

Sis, I want to encourage you to practice self-care on this adventure of living sober-minded. Because what you're doing is *brave*. It's brave to move beyond wanting something to actually *committing* to achieving it.

So it's no secret that steamy, hot, fragrant baths make my soul happy. But for you, it might be something else. I encourage you to find the self-care practice that feels like both a reward and a refreshment.

Here are some of the ways SoberMinded Sisters are practicing self-care:

- ✓ One woman gets up early to take a run as the sun is rising.
- ✓ One woman plans a trip to a tropical island for just herself!
- ✓ One woman takes the time to chop all the ingredients to make her favorite salad.
- ✓ One woman plans a hike for herself and her friends.
- ✓ One woman treats herself to a mani-pedi.
- ✓ One woman—who's thrilled to be hangover-free—signs up for an Ironman triathlon. (I know, I know. This doesn't have everyone's name on it.)
- ✓ One woman signs up for an oil painting class. (Do your research, because some of these are also drinking classes. Lol.)

If you're busy pouring out and giving to everyone else in your life, I want you to know that self-care is most important! You're taking care of yourself so you can give from a place of overflow. I used to think that self-care was nothing more than a choice to spend a bunch of money on spa services. But I discovered that it's really about finding a consistent practice that can be incorporated into daily life. I'll admit that a cursory review of the list above does reveal that a number of these things cost *dollars*. Fair.

But before you count yourself out because your budget is tight, let's talk about dollars. Because the woman who's drinking a $10 to $15 bottle of wine on a regular basis is shelling out a minimum of $300 on alcohol each month. Add in the drinks she buys when she's not at home, and she's at $350+. Sis, you know what you could do with that $350? A lot.

Despite the *similarities in sound*, self-care and selfishness are different. Self-care is not self*ish*. It's loving. It's responsible. It's healthy. And it's not even all about *you*. Your self-care practices benefit your family, your coworkers, and your friends who are blessed by you when you protect and nurture yourself. When you do that, you're giving from a place of abundance and not burnout.

I know you're facing your own unique challenges, Sis. Whether they're relational, emotional, physical, or financial, it's likely you're carrying a lot. And that's why it's so very important for you to take the time and energy (and possibly dollars) to invest in yourself.

No one else is going to make self-care a priority for you. I encourage you to invest in this kind of rest and renewal so that you can continue to be the very best version of yourself.

Just because life feels like a roller coaster, it doesn't mean I have to numb out for the highs and lows.

Building Resilience

People ask me all the time how I stay motivated. I don't. I stay consistent. When things get hard and I want to quit, that's when I keep going. The only way to "fail" in this sober-minded journey is to quit trying. *Resilience* is defined as the capacity to withstand or recover quickly from difficulties. I can say, with humility, that my resilience has deepened significantly since putting down the alcohol. It wasn't that long ago that drinking seemed like a dependable companion helping me face difficulties. I subconsciously viewed it as a "helper" when I felt overwhelmed or doubted myself.

Like the time I was surprised by a group of extended family popping into town for an overnight stay. I was happy to see them, but I felt insecure because my house was a mess from homeschooling all day and I didn't feel very "put together." I wasn't confident in myself, but I *was* certain that wine would instantly slow my racing heart, temporarily comfort me, and even give me a dose of confidence! And for a moment, it did!

But here's the catch: although alcohol *postponed* my feelings, it didn't *change* anything. It provided quick relief, but not true confidence or inner peace. Ultimately, my "quick fix" undermined my courage and weakened my inner resilience. It dulled everything all at once, including my ability to stand firm, trust in the ultimate Source of my strength, and stay present in the midst of uncertainty. Every time something challenging happened in my life, I was reinforcing the belief that I couldn't handle it without my "helper."

Friend, this was "the point" where I knew alcohol would lead me to places I didn't want to go if I didn't make a mindful change. And part of that change was having the courage to be uncomfortable by staying present to feelings I'd rather avoid: sadness, fear, anger, and more.

Part of living sober-minded is learning how to feel all the feels and fighting the urge to "outsource" our resilience to an elixir or anything else that ultimately undermines our best. Today I can look back and see that, at times, I leaned into alcohol as a crutch to "hold me up" when my intense emotions or circumstances felt like too much. The problem is that the more I depended on alcohol, the less resilient I became. (Truly, before I chose to start drinking, I was fierce. I had robust resources. I was mostly winning at life.) Once I began turning to alcohol, I was using that "escape hatch" more than I'd ever intended to.

People who are resilient have things in common: resourcefulness, good problem-solving skills, and a sense of empowerment. The number *one* thing that resilient people have in common is they are more likely to reach out for support when they need it, and they have a community full of support and connection.

Today, though, I know for sure I can do hard things. I can endure uncomfortable things. I can face life with all of its ups and downs. It wasn't easy to get here. I went through the fire. But I know it's possible to stay present when we don't want to. Just because life feels like a roller coaster, it doesn't mean I have to numb out for the highs and lows. I'm still learning in real time how to trust God and enjoy the ride.

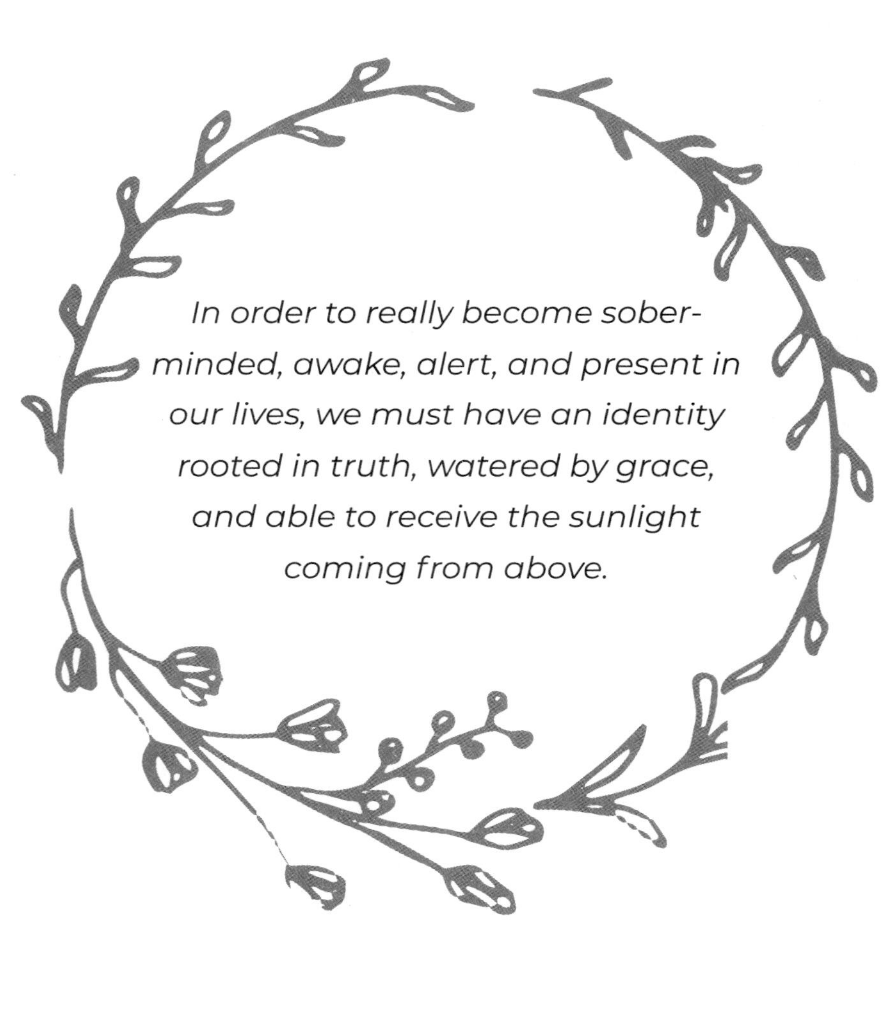

In order to really become sober-minded, awake, alert, and present in our lives, we must have an identity rooted in truth, watered by grace, and able to receive the sunlight coming from above.

True Identity

Do you wear masks?

I don't mean those fun pampering face masks to treat your skin. I mean the kind that covers (or even hides) your true essence. Some masks say: *I'm in control; I'm not afraid; I don't care; I'm not hurt;* or *I've got it all together*. We fear if we take these masks off, we might be met with judgment or disappointment. Part of this sober-minded journey is stepping into your authenticity, being seen for who you really are. The way we see ourselves matters; we live out of our identity.

It was a normal Wednesday evening, and our kids had a lot of projects due. Everyone was counting down to the Christmas break. I had started my spaghetti dinner around 5 p.m. and that also meant I had started a bottle of red wine at that time too. I knew millions of moms were doing the exact same thing around the globe—or at least that's what I had seen on TV and heard from my girlfriends. It was the "witching hours" of 5 to 8 p.m. I was navigating through being the mom of fickle teenagers and attempting connection with a busy husband. I had been my own person all day, but now I wasn't sure who I was. If I'm honest, I was trying to find my place in my own family. Engaged mom? (Yes, but not too engaged.) Referee between siblings? Attentive wife attuned to my husband's needs?

After sipping on the first glass of wine while the sauce simmered, it was easy to pour a bit more when my hubs was running late. After dinner, I poured a little bit more just to make cleaning the kitchen a bit more "fun." It was *there,* on my third glass, standing over the kitchen sink, that I realized I was getting smaller. I was shrinking back from my true identity as an individual. I quieted my voice, not really sharing my opinions. I didn't see them as that valuable. I was going along to get along. I was escaping the conflict and the lack of purpose and passion I had in my own life. Don't get me wrong, I love my family and the home we've built together. I was just having an identity "crisis" because I was wearing masks to protect myself and keep everyone happy. Do I have any fellow "people pleasers" out there? I was behaving out of my beliefs about myself. I looked for outside messages to confirm my internal beliefs, and, of course, when I went looking, I found them every time.

Let's face it. We all desire meaning in our lives. It begins early on as we search for significance and acceptance externally when really the journey is getting back to who we are intrinsically . . . not *what* we do, but *who* we are. We attempt to find this identity by over-giving, over-performing, and all of the other "overs"! We forget that we are worthy and have incredible value simply by virtue of being alive!

When I first began shifting away from mindless sipping in the evenings, I had to challenge my beliefs and I also had to practice genuine self-compassion. I started changing the way I related to myself in my own mind. I was more kind to myself than harsh, and I was basing more of my identity on the truth of the way our Creator sees us—and not just in theory, but in a deeper love relationship. I went back to my roots of believing *who* I was based on *Whose* I was.

A bedrock of my "why" for wanting change in my life goes back to wholehearted living. I didn't want to be torn in two with a divided mind or a dual identity. The duplicity in my life was sometimes painful. Seriously, sometimes it felt like I was one person by day and another by night. Masks of protection on throughout the day and then using a drink (or three) to wriggle them off at night . . . only to create someone I didn't always recognize.

In order to really become sober-minded, awake, alert, and present in our lives, we must have an identity rooted in truth, watered by grace, and able to receive the sunlight coming from above. You're worth it, Sister, just as you are!

We were not meant
to do this alone.

The Value of Community

When my girlfriend Rachel was in the hospital giving birth to her first child, the hours were dragging on and that child was *not* coming out. Her pain was excruciating. Rachel's husband was by her side, but he would admit that he had no way of *truly* understanding what it felt like to bring a human being into the world!

"Knock, knock."

Turning toward the door, Rachel recognized her closest girlfriend, Jasmine, a mom of three.

"Jazzy!" she hollered, welcoming the distraction and the friend.

"Let's do this, girl," Jasmine coached. And as someone who'd had some recent experience to draw from, Jasmine accompanied her friend, alongside Rachel's husband, through the rest of the delivery. She knew how it felt. She knew what helped. She knew what didn't help. Rachel needed someone who knew, intimately, what she was going through.

I've heard it said that there are two types of understanding. The first is when you have personally experienced what someone else is going through; that's called "type one" understanding. There's a strong sense of identification and empathy. The second type of understanding is offered with good intent but without direct identification with what the other person is feeling or experiencing because you have not dealt with it yourself, firsthand, so we call that "type two" understanding. In the above example, Rachel's husband was supporting his wife the best he could with "type two" understanding. When Jasmine entered the room, she brought with her "type one" understanding from having shared the same experience. Both were valuable.

When we're on the journey of alcohol-free living, we need the support of those who've walked the same path. Who've felt the same discomfort. Who know what helps and what hurts. We really benefit when we gain support from like-minded people with lots of "type one" understanding.

But when we try to do it on our own, we'll likely stay stuck.

When we isolate, we're more likely to give in to the relentless voices in our heads that are bullying us to drink.

When we isolate, we may give in to self-pity, believing we're the only ones who are having this experience.

When we isolate, we create a breeding ground for shame.

When we isolate, when we don't have a comrade to share with, we're more likely to believe the madness that marketers are selling us.

We were made for so much more.

For years, I tried to change my drinking on my own through willpower, rules, deprivation, and even talking negatively to myself: "Jenn, try harder, don't do that again." It didn't work. In that season I needed to know that I was normal, that it wasn't my fault, and that I wasn't alone in my struggle at wine o'clock. Thankfully I found some online connection and encouragement, but I needed more. I needed a place where I could build real relationships. We were not meant to do this alone, and that's why it wasn't working!

As a sober-minded sisterhood, we are stronger together than we ever were apart. Connection is the secret sauce of Sober Sis because having others normalize our experience and having a variety of people to process with are where the real growth comes. We have an exceptional amount of "type one" understanding!

The key to my progress in my relationship to alcohol hinged on moving from isolation to connection. Every day I'd be battered by this mental tug-of-war: "Will I drink

tonight? Will I have one? Will I have three? Do I really want it at all?" Sis, the chatter was absolutely exhausting. It was like this constant ping-pong match in my head that no one knew about.

And then, they did.

Now the Sober Sis community encourages me every single day. And we're all here for you, too. Sober Sis is a training ground for you to exercise the muscles needed to own your own decision and grow with support. You can do this!

Let us join you.

The SoberSis Highway

Free Guide

To download our free guide that reveals five successful strategies to skipping the wine tonight and feeling great in the morning, visit www.sobersis.com/get-free-guide.

21 Day Reset Challenge is the on-ramp to the "SoberSis highway." It is designed for women of all ages, backgrounds, and stories to experience taking an intentional break from alcohol without labels, judgment, or shame. This reset is ideal for women who are "sober curious," feel stuck in the detox-to-retox loop, and want to become the best version of themselves. The conversation and tools are geared for the "gray area" of the drinking spectrum. The "secret sauce" of SoberSis is our connection. We are a diverse group and yet find that we are like-minded in pursuing a holistic approach by incorporating mind, body, and spirit as keys to lasting and sustainable wholehearted living. Together we aspire to live in freedom and authenticity and to unlock the gift of being more present in our own lives! To join our next 21 Day Reset, use the following QR Code.

Alcohol-Free Lifestyle Course, also known as "AFL," is a 10-week online course designed for women who have participated in a 21 Day Reset and who desire more opportunity to practice alcohol-free living with daily guidance and small group support. This experience will keep momentum moving forward as well as give you the tools to keep from slipping backward into old habits and ways of thinking. Like everything else in SoberSis, it's about progress over perfection. Direction matters more than speed! The focus of this group is discovering the joys and benefits of alcohol-free living, while learning skills to stay present, socialize, and feel the feels!

The Quest is designed for a community of SoberMinded Sisters committing to continue this amazing journey to Awakened FREEDOM. While the AFL Course is the foundational course for building an alcohol-free lifestyle, The Quest takes those pillars and applies them to real life in a safe and supported community of application, accountability, and continued learning, while always celebrating progress over perfection. It's time to "take this show on the road!" In this group, we are like-minded and committed to celebrating "small" wins and huge milestones, sharing struggles, and always looking at every experience as another alcohol-free opportunity!

To learn more about Jenn, follow her on social media!

JennKautsch.com

Facebook @sobermindedsister

Instagram @SoberSis